I0408503

CONTENTS

PASSIVE INCOME NOW!

Your Action Plan For Financial Freedom

Unlocking the Secrets to Effective Wealth Generation through Passive Earning Strategies

By
Emily Richmond
And
Ahjan Samvara

For more information, or to book an event, contact :

ahjansamvara@gmail.com

https://www.ashirameditation.org

ISBN - Paperback: 9798859424047

First Edition: 10/5/2023

ABOUT THE AUTHORS

Emily Richmond

An esteemed thought leader on financial independence, Emily Richmond has devoted years to mastering the art of passive income streams. Continually seeking and analyzing the best strategies for financial freedom, Emily Richmond has successfully created an investment portfolio that now drives their passive income to sustain a financially free lifestyle. Leveraging this firsthand expertise, they provide their audiences with comprehensive resources to understand, evaluate, and implement passive income strategies. Their commitment to simplifying complex financial narratives has established them as an authority backer to both novices and the seasoned investors alike.

Ahjan Samvara

Ahjan Samvara is a distinguished meditation and mindfulness teacher, techno-visionary, prosperous businessman, and martial arts instructor. He is an embodiment of holistic success and mindfulness who upholds the belief that enlightenment lies within one's self and day-to-day life. Having instructed in Buddhist mysticism for over two decades, Samvara has successfully addressed all aspects of modern life - in work, school, sports, friendship, relationships, and even in leisure activities such as scuba diving.

As a pioneer in the technology industry, he successfully melds mindfulness and connectivity, leveraging his vast technical expertise to broaden his teachings' reach. His established businesses serve as real-world applications of his methodologies – exhibiting how mindfulness practices can be used to achieve not only spiritual but career success as well.

Moreover, as a martial arts instructor and a SCUBA instructor, Samvara teaches how different physical activities promote focus and discipline, aiding in the journey toward mindfulness and achievement. His teachings, coupled with his travels, have facilitated the sharing of diverse practices and experiences, profoundly influencing followers worldwide. Altogether, these credentials validate Samvara as an authority in translating spiritual principles into tangible success.

FOREWORD

Passive income has long been billed as the holy grail of financial freedom – a constant trickle of revenue that ideally involves little effort on the recipient's part. However, generating passive income is anything but passive. It requires strategy, intellect, and a whole lot of effort. The book you hold in your hand is a comprehensive guide to tap into the diverse world of passive income and enable you to achieve the coveted financial freedom.

The principles in this book are designed to make you rethink your approach to income. They are proven strategies for generating a substantial income, giving you the freedom to live life on your terms. Whether you're a seasoned investor looking to diversify your income streams or a beginner seeking a starting point in the world of passive income, this book is your roadmap to ultimate financial freedom.

INTRODUCTION

Welcome to Passive Income Now! Your Action Plan For Financial Freedom. This book is not merely a guide—it's a transformative journey, a holistic approach to attaining success based on your unique skills, aspirations, and vision. This is not about fitting into a preconceived notion of success, but about carving your pathway to prosperity.

This book combines efficient passive income strategies with a revolutionary approach towards personal wealth creation. The overarching theme outlines how to unleash the untapped potential within you—a potent force capable of manifesting an affluent life of financial independence and personal satisfaction—giving you the tools and strategies to chart your course towards your unique version of success.

In the subsequent sections, we will delve into three key strategies—Diversified Investing, Career Revolution, and Inner Wealth Unlocking—and explore their interconnectedness in unlocking your financial freedom. By the end of this journey, you'll have discovered ways to cultivate multiple income streams, revolutionize your career, align financial decisions with personal fulfillment, and re-imagine your financial journey.

The path towards financial freedom and personal satisfaction, while challenging, is profoundly rewarding. So plug in, dear reader, as we embark together on this journey. Buckle up for an adventure that promises to change the way you view money, work, and success. Let's begin our exploration on creating and following your uniquely curated pathway to success and financial freedom.
Our action plan is all about putting your knowledge into practice. After digging deep into your desires, skills, and potentials, charting your pathway to success, and cultivating your income streams, it's now time to get down to the nitty-gritty—creating and implementing

your personalized action plan. This chapter will guide you in aligning your endeavors with your passion and finance, harmonizing your lifestyle with your work, and maintaining an unshakeable inner harmony amidst economic uncertainties.

By the end of this action plan, you will be well-equipped to harmonize your passive income strategies, drastically revolutionize your career, and unlock unprecedented wealth from within. Your journey to financial freedom and personal satisfaction, powered by passive income, begins here! Are you ready?

CHAPTER 1: PASSIVE INCOME FOR FINANCIAL FREEDOM: PAVING THE WAY TO PROSPERITY

Imagine a life where your earnings are not directly tied to the hours you work, where you have the freedom to pursue your passions and enjoy life without worrying about making ends meet. Welcome to the world of passive income, the golden key to financial freedom.

Did you know that 63% of millionaires attribute their wealth to passive income? This surprising fact is not common knowledge, but it illuminates an interesting pathway towards wealth creation and financial freedom.

This book is for anyone desiring to break free from the rigid 9-5 working model, feeling the pinch of the daily commute, endless meetings, and the exasperation of living paycheck-to-paycheck. We will tackle your skepticism head-on—you may wonder if it's really possible to earn without actively working or whether this path is fraught with risks.

Dive into Passive Income for Financial Freedom is no ordinary piece of literature. Unlike other financial self-help books, we delve into the nitty-gritty of multiple passive income avenues, equipping you with practical tools for your wealth creation journey. The audience in focus – the dreamers, the go-getters, the hopefuls, who are ready to rewrite their financial stories.

In a world increasingly embracing digital technology, the time for passive income is now. The digital age offers myriad opportunities, low entrance barriers, and the ushering in of a global market.

Find courage in every chapter, strategy in every scenario, and motivation in each success story. This book brings you one step closer to taking charge of your financial destiny. Be ready for a detailed exploration of realistic and tested strategies that pave the way to financial freedom.

Leave skepticism at the door and open your mind to infinite possibilities. The path may be paved with challenges, but the rewards are equally great—financial freedom, peace of mind, and time to truly live your life.

No more waiting, no more wondering. Let's start this journey towards financial freedom right here, right now. After all, time is money, and in this case, your ticket to a prosperous, passive-income driven life.

CHAPTER 2: THE MIRAGE OF SET AND FORGET: DEBUNKING THE MYTH OF EFFORTLESS PASSIVE INCOME

Making money while you sleep has a beautiful ring to it. That's the idea behind passive income. But, as with any good thing, there's always a catch. Simply perceiving passive income as a 'get rich quick' scheme can leave you worse off. - Paraphrased from Robert Kiyosaki

At the core of our exploration is the myth of easy money and the couple of lessons that seem to escape the eager novice in the world of investing and financial independence. This chapter will reveal why passive income is not as passive as you might initially believe, and why financial freedom requires more than a cursory engagement with your investments. A wake-up call for those charmed by the seemingly effortless allure of passive income, here we challenge the commonly held belief and unmask the reality often glossed over in casual conversations.

The problem of passive income for financial freedom hinges on several dimensions that are critical to the understanding and execution of this financial strategy. Firstly, the major issue is the initial requirement for a substantial investment, be it time, money or both. Though passive income is designed to circulate returns without the need for active input, getting to that stage often means investing a significant amount of resources in the beginning. In this context, it is worthwhile to mention that introducing a new business, buying rental property, or investing in the stock market, can be high-cost ventures that serve to deter potential investors.

Conceptually, understanding passive income can also pose as a problem. Many fall under the misconception that passive income requires no work, which is untrue. It certainly requires less work after it is set but nothing is truly 'passive'. It takes patience, dedication, and adjustments based on the evolution of the market— a process that can be overwhelming for even the most seasoned investor. Balancing the active involvement needed and the passive nature of the returns is a precise science that few truly master.

Then comes the problem of risk tolerance. Passive income investments carry a reasonable amount of risk. These risks could be related to the market, economic trends, or even changes in the law. Each factor makes passive income generation a risk-reward proposition that can be daunting to handle for some. Understanding these risks and knowing how to navigate them is the key to achieving financial freedom.

Another inherent problem is the time it takes for passive income streams to mature into substantial yields. Unlike active income where results are relatively immediate, passive income can take years or even decades to become significant. This is not a method for those seeking quick financial gains, but rather, it is a long-term approach that prioritizes sustainability over speed.

Finally, tax and legal complications form a dimension that many overlook. Passive income methods can have different tax implications compared to the traditional income streams. In addition, there may be legal hurdles that need to be cleared before the income stream can be established. Knowing how to manage these potential hindrances, and seeking appropriate advice when necessary, is crucial in using passive income as a tool for achieving financial freedom.

In summary, while passive income has the potential to provide financial freedom, navigating the issues including the initial investment, understanding the concept and risk, patience needed, and tax and legal issues, needs careful planning and execution.

Passive income is seen as a crucial aspect when it comes to achieving financial freedom. It refers to making money without ongoing effort, unlike the conventional method of receiving payment for active working hours. The interest of people towards passive income is driven by the desire for financial freedom, which is the ability to maintain your desired lifestyle without the need to work for an income. This type of financial situation can provide an unmatchable level of flexibility and security.

The concept of passive income, however, comes with its set of challenges. First and foremost, establishing a passive income source is not an easy task. Whether it's rental income, dividends, or business income, it requires intensive initial effort, strategic planning, and sometimes even substantial capital. It is hardly ever a case of simple, immediate return on investment. The misconception that earning passive income is fast and easy often leads to disappointments.

Another pressing issue is the risk associated with many passive income sources. While they have great potentials, they are also quite vulnerable. The revenue from rental properties, for example, is not always guaranteed. You may witness periods with no tenants or face repair expenses, damaging your returns. Investments can be volatile, fluctuating with market trends. Therefore, while they can bring substantial returns, they can also lead to significant losses. It's important to understand these risks and consider them carefully in the strategy.

Another aspect to consider is the tax implications. The earnings received from various kinds of passive income, like rental income, royalties, and dividends, can have different tax treatments. Understanding these tax obligations is vital to ensure compliance and adequately calculate the net income expected from these sources.

Lastly, while the idea of passive income revolves around the concept of 'making money while you sleep', it doesn't mean there is no effort involved. It often requires regular updates, monitoring, and sometimes, interventions to ensure its continuous profitability and sustainability.

Despite these issues, the pursuit of passive income sources is still a wise and profitable endeavour if approached carefully. With ample amount of research, careful planning, due diligence, and prudent risk management, passive income can truly become a path to financial freedom. Remember that patience here is a virtue. The process will take time and effort, but it has the potential to provide stability and prosperity in your financial life.

Firstly, the problem of passive income for financial freedom can cause stress and lifestyle alterations. People who rely on fixed, active incomes often find themselves working incredibly long hours, sacrificing their personal time and relationships to meet their financial targets. This constant pressure and absence of free time can lead to high levels of stress, mental fatigue, and eventually burnout, significantly affecting a person's overall well-being and happiness. Altered lifestyle is another consequence as these individuals may find themselves unable to afford luxuries or non-essential items that enrich daily living, hence making them prone to frustration and dissatisfaction.

Secondly, it can suppress ambitions and dreams creating a monotonous life. Passive income provides the financial freedom that allows people to pursue their passions, hobbies, and dreams without worrying about immediate financial obligations. However, a lack of passive income channels might force individuals to compromise on their ambitions, big or small, to ensure they stay financially stable. This limits the scope of personal growth, exploration, and can lead to a life dominated by monotony, thereby decreasing overall life satisfaction.

Lastly, the absence of passive income can lead to financial insecurity that might affect future decisions. Building passive income is popularly recognized as an effective strategy for achieving long-term financial security. However, without passive income, individuals are often limited to their regular earnings, which might be barely enough to handle daily expenses, let alone unexpected emergencies or retirement planning. This financial insecurity can place a considerable burden on people, forcing them into anxiety about their future, and driving them to make decisions they might not prefer such as refraining from bigger investments, or delaying important events like retirement. As a result, the problem of passive income and financial freedom deeply impacts an individual's personal life, aspirations, and future security, underscoring the need for diversified income streams.

Passive income is income that requires minimal labor to earn and maintain. It is also referred to as residual income. Having multiple income streams can change your life in several ways:

1. Financial Security: Passive income can bring a sense of financial security. You're no longer solely reliant on your main job to cover expenses, as your passive income sources can provide that extra cushion against life's ups and downs.

2. Financial Freedom: By building a quality passive income, you can achieve financial freedom. It allows you to retire early or leave a job you don't enjoy without financial worries. Also, you can use this income to fund your goals, whether they are traveling, starting a new business, or buying a home.

3. Time Flexibility: It's income that doesn't tie you down to a specific location or require you to work particular hours. Once systems are in place, passive income allows you to earn money while you're sleeping, on vacation, or spending time with family.

4. Compound Growth: Many passive income methods allow your earnings to grow over time, especially when it comes to investments. This compounding effect can result in significant wealth growth.

5. Legacy: Finally, passive income streams can also be a legacy that you can give to your children or beneficiaries. Instead of leaving

behind a one-time lump sum, passive income can continue to provide for them indefinitely.

Therefore, if you care about financial security, freedom, and flexibility, it's crucial to consider building passive income streams.

Passive income, or residual income, holds great significance due to the multiple ways it can impact and improve your life. Firstly, passive income can give you a profound sense of financial security. When you have a reliable passive income, you aren't just dependent on your primary job to cover all your expenses. You have an extra financial cushion to lean on in times of unpredictability or financial instability.

Additionally, passive income not only ensures financial security but can also lead to financial freedom. Imagine being able to retire early or leave a job that you don't love, all just because you have a solid passive income. This extra income source can then be used to fulfil various dreams, like travelling the world, launching a new business, or owning a house.

Not just that, passive income also provides you with the gift of time. You're not bound by location or working hours when it comes to earning passive income. You can be making money even whilst you're sleeping, holidaying, or just spending a quality day with your loved ones.

Passive income also grows over time, especially when it comes to investments. This compound growth not only gives you more money over time but also leads to significant wealth creation.

Lastly, remember that passive income is a legacy you can pass down to future generations. It's a constant flow of income that continues to provide for your dear ones long after you're gone, instead of just a one-time lump sum of money.

For instance, the story of Pat Flynn, a well-known entrepreneur, and podcast host, serves as a compelling real-life example. He was laid off from his job in 2008, but rather than finding another job, he decided to work on his passive income project – a website he'd created to help people pass an architecture exam. The website started making $8,000 a month, and Flynn never needed to get a traditional job again (Smart Passive Income). This example serves as a testament to how passive income can give you time flexibility, financial security, and ultimate freedom.

In essence, if you value financial security, the freedom of choice and time, then the significance of incorporating passive income can't be overstated. It's an investment in your future - one that could lead to life-changing benefits.

Firstly, dealing with passive income for financial freedom isn't an endeavor you embark upon lightly. I understand that it comes with its unique set of challenges, such as the difficulty in finding the right investment or platform to invest in and earning consistent returns from it. It's not a simple task, and deciding where to put your hard-earned money can be a nerve-wracking process, often filled with uncertainty and fear of the unknown.

Secondly, I grasped the frustration that stems from the lack of immediate results. Just like planting a tree, developing a passive income stream demands time, patience, and nurturing. It may take weeks, months, or even years to start seeing substantial returns. This waiting period can become a trying time, where you may begin questioning your actions and decisions, creating an intense internal struggle with self-doubt and apprehension.

Lastly, there's the inherent struggle associated with maintaining and managing numerous passive income streams. Balancing your time between your different investments as well as your personal life and career can be extremely overwhelming. It requires you to be adept at multitasking and juggling different duties, which can add pressure and lead to burnout.

Knowing these struggles, I'm here to tell you that there's a solution to ease your path towards financial freedom. I aim to provide guidance that will tackle these struggles and serve as a roadmap, transforming these challenges into stepping stones. In the forthcoming chapters, I will succinctly delve into these solutions. Then, I'll teach you how to enact each step, detailing a comprehensive approach tailored to improve your journey towards financial independence.

CHAPTER 3: BUILDING A PASSIVE INCOME PORTFOLIO: YOUR PATHWAY TO FINANCIAL FREEDOM

Financial freedom is available to those who learn about it and work for it. - Robert Kiyosaki

Welcome to this crucial chapter - Building a Passive Income Portfolio: Your Pathway to Financial Freedom! As we explore the fascinating and potentially life-changing world of passive income, remember the words of Robert Kiyosaki. Working towards financial freedom necessitates learning and consistent action.

To start with, let's clear the air on what exactly passive income means. Passive income refers to the earnings derived from a rental property, limited partnership, or other enterprises in which a person is not actively involved. It has often been said that the wealthy work differently than the rest, but really, they just make their money work differently.

The beauty of passive income, as the name implies, is that it doesn't require your active participation all the time. Once the initial effort is put into setting up the income source, the money flows in with little need for active maintenance. Imagine earning while you sleep, vacation, or spend time with your family. That's precisely what passive income can do.

In this chapter, we will guide you through the process of identifying potential passive income streams, setting them up, and effectively maintaining your portfolio for sustained financial success. By building a diverse and robust portfolio of passive income sources, you will create a safety net that can carry you towards financial freedom. But the question is - how?

Stay tuned, as we dive deep into exploring the strategies, tips, and tricks needed to build a solid passive income portfolio to secure your financial future.

Uncovering a mind-blowing solution to passive income for financial freedom requires an innovative approach, creativity, dedicated research, and a heavy pinch of risk-taking. Here we will dive into two key strategies: low-input high-yield ventures and leveraging upcoming technological trends.

Firstly, consider low-input high-yield investments, typified by real estate investments. Rental properties are a prime example of passive income, where following initial investment and minimal oversight, a regular income stream is generated. Furthermore, home-sharing platforms have made this more accessible than ever before. It's not just about homes and apartments either. Think outside the box - renting out your parking space, a piece of vacant land for events or farming, or even storage space offers multiple routes for passive income.

Another example is peer-to-peer lending platforms. With these services, you play the role of a bank, lending your money in return for regular interest payments. The risk varies, and therefore the return does too, hence diversification across multiple loans is key.

Secondly, leverage upcoming technological trends. The increasing digitalization of our world opens new avenues for passive income. Create a smartphone app, or invest in someone who can. Once developed and published, an app can be a consistent income source as it's downloaded or makes ad revenue.

Alternatively, consider e-commerce. Dropshipping businesses can be created with relatively low initial investment. Here, you're selling products directly to the consumer without holding inventory. Your only job is to manage the online storefront and customer service whilst a third-party handles the inventory and shipping logistics.

Lastly, investing in cryptocurrency staking may yield considerable returns. By participating in the validation process of transactions, you earn more of the same cryptocurrency. It's crucial to be cautious and well-informed about potential risks and market volatility, as this isn't a guaranteed profit and can lead to losses.

As you explore these methods and more, remember the golden rule of a mind-blowing passive income: diversify. By spreading your investment over various opportunities, you generate multiple income streams that could stand independent of each other. This way, should one falter, others are there to keep the income flowing. Moreover, you also increase chances for higher returns and protect the sustainability of your financial freedom.

In conclusion, the key to unlocking mind-blowing passive income is innovation, exploitation of new technological trends, diversification, and the courage to take calculated risks. These principles set the foundation for robust and successful financial freedom.

An untapped domain of generating a passive income is through content creation. For instance, once a blog, website, or YouTube channel is established, monetizing these platforms can provide a steady revenue stream. With YouTube, ad revenue and sponsorships can be highly profitable, especially with a loyal subscriber base. For written content, affiliate marketing can be a key element where product recommendations can generate income from purchases.

Another approach is self-publishing e-books or online courses. In the ongoing age of digital learning, there is a high demand for educational material online. Once published, these digital products continue to bring in revenue without any additional efforts.

In a similar line, creating digital assets like copyright-free photographs, digital art or designs could also generate income, especially through online marketplaces like Shutterstock or Etsy. An initial investment of time and effort can lead to prolonged returns as these assets are licensed or sold.

Investing in stocks and shares also has potential. Dividend-generating stocks provide regular payouts aside from the potential for value appreciation which make for a substantial passive income source over time. Careful, proactive research before investing is highly critical in this case to safeguard your financial health.

REITs- Real Estate Investment Trusts provide another potential investment avenue where you invest in mortgage-backed securities, commercial real estates, or pools of properties. As per law, they are required to pay out most of their taxable profits to shareholders as dividends, making them an interesting source of passive income.

Remember, each passive income stream comes with its degrees of risk and return, and no strategy fits all. One must carefully evaluate the pros and cons of each approach, consider their financial position, skills, time commitment, and risk tolerance before plunging into any passive income adventure.

When discussing the limitations of the prevailing mindset, it's essential to note that many people associate passive income only with property rentals or stock investments, negating the vast array of possibilities offered by the digital age. The mentality of limiting one's financial streams to primary employment versus investing in multiple sources of income can affect individuals' financial growth potential.

Research supports this by revealing that the wealthiest individuals invest in various income sources. According to Tom Corley's Rich Habits studies, the majority of self-made millionaires adopted the practice of creating multiple revenue streams. A staggering 65% of them had three streams, 45% had four, and 29% had five or more.

Not fully understanding and leveraging the potential of the technological revolution to build new income sources, such as affiliate marketing, digital content creation, or e-course teaching, leads to missed opportunities. Moreover, the misconception that passive income requires no work or effort is misleading. Whether it's initial research, careful planning, or the setting up of a platform, effort and dedication are indeed required.

In contrast, another approach exists - the antithesis, which suggests not seeking additional income at all. This minimalist perspective highlights the importance of reducing desires, needs, and expectations to achieve financial freedom. It pictures income from an entirely different standpoint, propagating the idea that fewer needs translate into less income required, thus leading to a simpler yet content life.

These contrasting mindsets present different paths to financial flexibility. Both have merits and downsides, requiring careful consideration and an understanding of one's financial goals, lifestyle preferences, and risk tolerance. While a diversified income might bring in more money, it likely involves more initial input and ongoing management. Meanwhile, the minimalist approach requires strict limits on spending and lifestyle choices.

Striking a balance between these aspects, tailoring them to one's unique financial situation, and aligning them with personal lifestyle goals could be the key to achieving financial freedom. The common denominator to these contrasting strategies is mindfulness and conscientious decision-making regarding one's financial health.

As the dawn gently unfolded, coating the city in a soft glimmer, Kendra sat, eyes twinkling with the hue of ambition, at her mahogany table. She had a firm resolution etched in her mind - she was going to acheive financial freedom, and she was going to do it unconventionally.

She swapped the safety of property rentals and the undulating waves of stock market turbulence for an uncharted territory, teeming with potential - the world of passive income in the digital realm.

To begin her journey, she developed an intriguing smartphone application, filling a niche she discovered through intensive market research. This new endeavor didn't require Kendra to become a tech wizard overnight. Rather, she partnered with techno-savvy individuals and brought her vision to life. As the application gained traction, downloads skyrocketed, creating a profitable flow of ad revenue.

Simultaneously, Kendra added a new feather to her business cap - dropshipping. With the rise of e-commerce, she found a reliable third-party supplier and established an online shopfront. Now, she was selling trendy products without the need of inventory management, generating an added stream of income with minimal effort.

Not one to become complacent, Kendra then moved to exploit the educational potential of the cyber world. A proficient baker, she compiled her knowledge into an online course, providing her fans and novices with a unique learning experience. With each course purchase, her bank account swelled, and the sweet taste of financial freedom became more apparent.

Yet, Kendra didn't stop at perpetuating the trend of diversification within her financial repertoire. She delved into the realm of cryptocurrency staking, leveraging it to generate returns. Cryptocurrency, she discovered, was more than just a buzzword; it was a tool that, if used wisely, could yield substantial rewards.

Success swept in as the fruits of Kendra's approach started compiling. Multiple sources of income began to yield rewards, creating a symphony of sustainable cash flow that no single stream of income could have promised. Kendra's formula was working; she discovered that financial freedom dances harmoniously with resourcefulness, curiosity, and a sense of adventure.

Throughout her journey, Kendra had learned the best lesson of all - diversification is the lifeline of passive income. It was this ethos that allowed her to create a robust and ever-evolving blueprint for financial success, changing her life and potentiality forever.

With one last look at her burgeoning account balance, Kendra leaned back and smiled. Her mission, precariously launched on the pivot of determination, had reached its zenith. Passive income wasn't a myth anymore; it was real, yielding and there for the taking, for anyone daring enough to venture out of their comfort zone.

Kendra's innovative approach to financial independence essentially tackled the problems of relying on single income and conventional investments. She creatively took control of her financial destiny by diving head-first into modern, digital forms of making money. By doing so, she not only diversified her income sources but reduced the risk associated with dependence on only one or two streams of revenues.

She leveraged the wonders of the digital world to derive passive income. She used her application idea to solve a niche problem for clients worldwide. As the idea clicked, people were not only willing to use it but her ad revenue also started pouring in. This shows how tackling real-world problems and devising plausible solutions in the digital realm can prove profitable.

Her dropshipping venture illustrated a different problem-solving approach. Instead of adhering to the issues of inventory management and delivery logistics, Kendra teamed up with a reliable third-party supplier. This step reduced her initial investment and risk. More importantly, it gave her the opportunity to focus on other aspects of the business like customer acquisition, marketing, and relationship building.

Her foray into online education was an inspirational example of creating a market for her existing skills. Teeming with knowledge in baking, Kendra dealt with the problem of limited local audience head-on. She went digital, imparting baking lessons globally. This helped in diversifying her income, and also demonstrated that pre-existing skills, if marketed rightly, can become a lucrative income stream.

Lastly, her plunge into cryptocurrency staking was a calculated move to further diversify. She avoided the age-old problems of traditional investing; instead, she embraced a modern method, understanding that the crypto assets not only kept her portfolio ahead of the curve, but it was also less likely to be influenced by economic downturns in the traditional market.

Through these ventures, Kendra didn't just create multiple income streams; she unlocked a sustainable, scalable, and profitable sphere of passive income. She solved the problem of financial dependency and insecurity using the digital arena's boundless possibilities. It was an eloquent testament that digital advancements, if tactfully explored, can transform our financial trajectory.

The embracing of an innovative financial approach, as Kendra did, ushers in multiple transformative advantages with profound implications for personal financial management. Firstly, it mitigates the risks tied to a single stream of income. By nurturing different sources of income, it acts as a safety net if one stream faces a downturn.

There's an inherent flexibility in this approach. Let's say you are an individual in a full-time job wanting to earn more. Besides the regular job, you could explore opportunities for tutoring online in your area of expertise. The online world has made it feasible to turn your skills or knowledge into an income stream through the creation of online resources, courses, or products.

Advancements in the digital sphere also present the vast arena of e-commerce that cannot be overlooked. You don't necessarily need to stock or deliver products for this. A dropshipping model, as Kendra employed, can scale with less stress compared to traditional retail businesses.

Unleashing creativity is another significant advantage that comes along with digital entrepreneurship. It lets you shape your career in potentially any direction you desire. For instance, if you feel intrigued by the possibilities of cryptocurrency, you can dabble in it and learn on the fly. You can start with simple investments and gradually move into complex areas like staking.

Research supports this approach. According to a report published in 2020 by Small Business Trends, the average millionaire has as many as seven streams of income. By diversifying this way, they spread their risk, make the most of their skills, and continuously capture new opportunities as they arise.

Investopedia also emphasizes diversification as a risk-management strategy. Essentially, the more areas you invest in, the less affected you are by a single market's volatility. It's one of the reasons why many young investors are progressively venturing into digital currencies. Reports from the Global Cryptocurrency Benchmarking Study reveal that the number of crypto wallets has seen a nearly tenfold increase in five years.

Substantiating further is the rise in the e-learning market, which is projected to reach $325 billion by 2025 as per Research and Markets. It reflects the massive potential lying dormant in our skills that we can exploit to our advantage. The surge in smartphone ownership, supporting app usage, adds another solid backing to the prospect of app-based income.

The advantages are manifold: reduced risk, increased income, greater resilience, and more personal satisfaction. Kendra's story compellingly demonstrates an untapped world of potentialities that only requires us to look at financial stability differently. A shift in perspective towards unorthodox sources of passive income, with subsequent diversification and leveraging of resources, can empower us to redefine our financial roadmaps and imagine possibilities we didn't think were possible.

The story of Tim Ferriss is an authentic and inspiring example of successfully creating diversified passive income streams. He is an entrepreneur, author, podcaster, and investor best known for his book, The 4-Hour Workweek. Ferriss's approach to passive income is built around the concept of 'lifestyle design', which dismisses the traditional 'work until retirement' model and promotes building a balanced lifestyle that incorporates work, play, and personal growth.

Understanding the power of digitalisation, Ferriss started out by automating his nutritional supplement business, BrainQUICKEN. Instead of personally handling all aspects of the business, he outsourced operations, customer service, and logistics to various companies around the world. Through the advanced use of email autoresponders, dropshipping, and eCommerce tools, he was able to reduce his active involvement in the business to only four hours a week. Despite this, the business continued making money, which he would reinvest into other ventures.

Ferriss then ventured into writing, creating the 4-Hour series of books, where he shares his knowledge on lifestyle design, fitness, and cooking. These became best sellers, generating substantial royalties. He also strategically used his books to build his personal brand which he then leveraged to successfully launch a blog and a podcast - The Tim Ferriss Show.

His blog and podcast, which often feature renowned guests from various fields, have millions of monthly listeners and readers. They generate income through sponsorships, advertising, and affiliate marketing. Ferriss also transformed some of the podcast episodes into an audiobook, Tools of Titans, which became another source of passive income.

Moreover, Ferriss has invested in several technology companies, including Uber, Facebook, Twitter, and Alibaba, providing him with significant returns. His investment strategy is to focus on early-stage tech startups in the digital and tech industry where he sees growth potential.

Each of these income streams leverages a common theme - Ferriss' commitment to optimizing, automating, and outsourcing to maximize efficiency and minimize active involvement. It demonstrates how embracing digitalization, personal branding, and strategic investments can create significant passive income streams.

In the grand tapestry of financial independence, Kendra masterfully illustrated how taking the digital leap can solve the conventional problems of economic insecurity. She embraced the digital world's capacity to serve as a platform for creative and innovative avenue having her smartphone application, embarking on a dropshipping venture, hosting an online baking course, or adventuring into cryptocurrency staking. Kendra demonstrated that these untraditional methods could, in fact, result in multiple streams of passive income.

The multifaceted approach not only diversified her revenue but also substantially reduced her financial risks. Each venture catered to a unique market potential. This considered holistic diversification safeguarded her financial future against the fluctuations of individual income streams.

More than financial gains, Kendra's digital voyage brought about a pronounced transformation in her personal and professional life. The confidence she gained boosted her mental well-being, culminating in reduced stress and better emotional stability. The improved financial situation also influenced her relationships, allowing for happier, more fulfilling interactions with her loved ones.

Professionally, the digital solutions Kendra pioneered significantly enhanced her entrepreneurial skills and opened unique avenues for further growth. She was revered for her problem-solving capabilities and innovative mindset. This journey wasn't just about achieving financial freedom. It symbolized the power of solving problems innovatively, of thinking outside the box, and daring to approach things differently. Kendra's story gives us hope, inspiring us to look beyond ordinary means and envision fresh and improved ways of achieving our goals.

CHAPTER 4: UNRAVELING THE SECRET: PASSIVE INCOME HORIZONS FOR FINANCIAL EMANCIPATION

Financial freedom is available to those who learn about it and work for it. - Robert Kiyosaki

As an acclaimed author Robert Kiyosaki puts it, there's no quick route to financial freedom. Notably, it is about learning, effort, and the determination to work towards it. So, let's take this journey together to explore and understand how a mind-blowing career solution can help you accomplish financial independence.

In the realm of financial emancipation, a popular notion revolves around mastering the craft of passive income generation. Passive income, an income channel that yields regular earnings with minimal or no ongoing activity, is becoming a much sought-after path for modern-day workers and entrepreneurs. This unchartered territory holds promises of financial stability and provides an escape from the typical 9-5 grind.

Now, the million-dollar question is, 'How can we transition from a wistful dream of passive income generation to a tangible reality?' It takes a strategic combination of proper planning, resolute determination, resource optimization, and most importantly, an innovative career solution that screams, 'mind-blowing.' Let's break it down and decipher this code.

Active participation and consistent efforts are the first steps towards establishing a successful career to earn passive income. Effort is a critical ingredient, especially at the beginning, as building a system that generates a steady cash flow, might demand an upfront investment of time, creative energy, and sometimes even finances. So, having a well-thought-out plan with clearly defined goals is absolutely essential.

Notably, selecting the right type of passive income venture can be influenced by factors such as your skills, interests, experiences, and the amount of the initial investment you're willing to put in. For instance, if you have always been an ardent reader and a passionate writer, writing a best-selling eBook could be your pathway to financial freedom. The digital revolution has made the distribution and sale of eBooks simpler than ever, allowing authors to reach a global audience and generate a substantial passive income.

In contrast, if numbers and market trends fascinate you, investment in stocks or bonds might yield you a steady passive income. It would be, however, wise to thoroughly understand the financial market, monitor investment trends, and make informed decisions. Alternatively, you could even consider starting your own blog revolving around a subject matter that you are passionate about. Once your blog garners significant traffic, you could monetize it through affiliate marketing, sponsored content or advertisements.

Though the allure of passive income seems gratifying, it's important to remember the associated risks. Not every investment will reap profits and not all ventures will ensure a smooth sail. Establishing a passive income source can involve a significant learning curve, vulnerable to mistakes and failures. However, adversity is just as much a teacher as success, providing valuable lessons to refine your strategy.

Seeking professional advice from experts, mentors, or financial advisors can also be highly beneficial. They can provide valuable insight, guide you on potential pitfalls, and help maximize your returns. Moreover, educating yourself is just as important. Numerous resources are available online and offline to provide essential knowledge and insights on passive income strategies.

As much as the concept of passive income involves freedom from the typical 9-5 job, it doesn't mean disconnecting yourself entirely from your income source. You'd need to stay actively involved, at least indirectly, to monitor and optimize your financial growth. It's necessary to review your chosen passive income venture's performance regularly and make adjustments as required.

Lastly, it's crucial to stay patient and keep a positive mindset. Success rarely shows up overnight - it's a journey with ups and downs. When setbacks present themselves, remember why you embarked on this path to begin with and let that inspire you to keep going. Financial independence through passive income is a marathon, not a sprint, and perseverance is your key to crossing the finish line.

In today's fast-paced world, the majority of people are still tied to a traditional conception of earning an income: working a regular job and receiving a paycheck in return. This is what we are encouraged to pursue from a young age, a script that has been deeply ingrained in societal expectations. You study hard, get a good job, work from 9 to 5, and look forward to the weekends and annual leave.

There is nothing inherently wrong with this approach. However, it comes with a variety of limitations and ignores the potential of passive income. Firstly, the typical work structure hinges on a direct exchange of time for money. This means that there's an upper limit to your potential earnings since there are only so many hours in a day. Add in the need for sleep, rest, leisure activities, and family time, the available hours for work decrease substantially.

Another limitation is that this mindset doesn't take significant advantage of the digital age and global economy. In an interconnected era, where technology has blurred geographical boundaries, opportunities to earn aren't limited to a physical workplace or specific hours. People halfway across the globe can access and pay for your product or service, meaning there's a vast audience out there who might be willing to part with their income to benefit from what you have to offer.

According to a report by prominent economist Thomas Piketty, capital income, which includes passive income from property, dividends, interest, and royalties, grows faster than income from labor. This means that the people who earn passive income are likely to become wealthier quicker than those who depend solely on labor income.

In his influential book, The Four-Hour Workweek, Timothy Ferriss points out that trading time for money is a paradigm that keeps many people trapped in an endless cycle of work. By relying heavily on this traditional mindset, one misses out on exploring potentially lucrative areas that require less time and effort.

Moreover, the traditional earning model often fails to consider financial resilience, particularly from unforeseen circumstances. An illness, job redundancy, or any other change in circumstances can severely affect the primary stream of income. Conversely, having multiple streams of passive income offers a safety net which can endure these unplanned instances.

There's a massive contrast between active and passive income in terms of wealth accumulation. While the traditional mindset of actively working for paychecks has its merits, people who generate passive income often see a faster movement toward financial freedom. This is because they're not trading their time for money anymore–their money is working for them instead. They've broken free from the limitations of conventional thinking and unlocked the potential of the modern, digital economy.

In conclusion, while one path isn't necessarily better than the other, it's crucial to understand that there are alternatives to the traditional work model that can lead to enhanced financial freedom and quality of life. The choice between simply living to work or capitalizing on passive income streams to create a life with more freedom and flexibility is highly individualistic and depends on each person's goals, priorities, and circumstances. Both paths demand diligence, patience, and a strategic approach–however, the path less trodden–passive income generation–promises a more enriching life journey to financial independence.

In the bustling labyrinth of life, a transformative career solution beams like a lighthouse, guiding individuals towards shores of financial liberty and professional fulfilment. Stepping off the well-trodden path, we find ourselves venturing into the traded realms of passive income and solopreneurship. Imagine crafting an innovative software solution, a groundbreaking application or an enthralling online course integrating your diverse skills, expertise and passion into an irresistible package. You allow users worldwide to access it for a fee and voila, a potential source of long term revenue materializes.

Admittedly, it takes an invigorating blend of inspiration, dedication, and precision to concoct such a solution. And if this doesn't fit your schema, why not consider subverting the common paradigms of real estate? Rather than investing in tangibles like urban living spaces, delve into the unchartered waters of virtual property, a thriving component of the digital universe. Virtual real estate, often associated with online games or digital worlds, holds the potential to generate significant ROI.

Yet, this narrative would be incomplete without emphasizing the significance of intellectual property. Best-selling books, popular poems, catchy lyrics, breathtaking photographs, artworks, unique inventions - these are all potent vehicles for creating wealth that should not be overlooked.

And finally, let's not lose sight of leveraging expertise. Offering online consultations and counselling sessions in your field of wisdom can be a rewarding and deep enriching enterprise. After all, knowledge is the only asset that enhances upon sharing.

So, enthralled by these revolutionary possibilities, as we sashay into the dawn of a new era, it's evident that the traditional norms of earning are gradually dissipating. The baton has passed on to us now, quelling the monotony of 9-to-5 jobs, the quest for truly mind-blowing career solutions begins. Converging on the cusp of ambition and creativity, let's write our own narratives of success, painting every nuance of the professional landscape with strokes of innovation, breaking norms, and establishing a new status quo that will stand the tests of time. Let's take a leap of faith beyond the typical, plunge into the intriguing depths of possibilities, and emerge with golden opportunities that not only sustain our hunger for wealth but also feed our souls with unmatched satisfaction. The journey may be fraught with trials, but the victory will indeed be sweet.

Harnessing the power of passive income and solopreneurship lies in their ability to meld work-life equilibrium with financial prosperity. When innovative digital products are developed, they can be continuously monetized long after the initial sweat equity is put in. For instance, you could put in countless hours creating an online course, but once it is complete, it can be sold to an endless number of consumers across the globe, thereby creating a reliable income stream that demands minor maintenance efforts.

Virtual real estate is another innovative avenue that holds untapped potential. As our world becomes increasingly digital, properties in virtual worlds are now being sold for thousands - sometimes even millions - of dollars. The stakeholders, by trading these assets or renting them to advertisers or users, can lucratively capitalize on this surreal dimension of the digital universe.

Intellectual property creation also presents lucrative career alternatives. Authoring a best-selling book, for example, not only earns you considerable royalty but further creates opportunities for branching out into related markets - be it speaking engagements, workshops, or movie deals. Similarly, poets, photographers, or even inventors can license their creative productions for use by others and enjoy the ensuing royalty. With their unique blend of creativity and legal protection against unauthorized use, these intellectual properties offer a promising alternative to traditional forms of income generation.

Additionally, the rise of the digital era affords specialists the chance to share their knowledge like never before. An expert in any field, with a working internet connection, can provide consultations, masterclasses, or counselling sessions to a global clientele. This elevates opportunities for income and allows the expert to build an international reputation while working from any location.

In our rapidly evolving world of work, the conventional jobs that once dominated are gradually making way for more innovative and novel career solutions. By leveraging creativity, passion, and our unique skills, we can redefine our professional trajectories. Doing so not only promises potentially superior financial returns but also a level of satisfaction and personal fulfilment that traditional jobs often fail to deliver.

In excavating further into the prospect of passive income and solopreneurship, it becomes evident that these ventures operate on the principle of 'work once, reap forever.' Introducing a successful digital commodity into the market primarily demands one's indispensable efforts during its ideation and creation phases. Still, once past this stage, without any notable endeavor, it cultivates recurring income. According to a research by Statista, eLearning market is projected to surpass $243 billion by 2022, demonstrating the broad scope this pathway holds.

The virtual real estate realm is another profitable hub to deliberate over. Investment in virtual landscapes, as peculiar as it may sound, is emerging as a legitimate business strategy. According to data from Nonfungible.com, the sale of virtual properties experienced a staggering boom in 2020, with a total value of trades exceeding $500 million. This illustrates the potential for virtual real estate to evolve into a mainstream investment option.

Creating intellectual property and translating it into passive income has dual benefits. On one hand, it gives individuals freedom to express their creativity, while on the other hand, it facilitates consistent income. Interestingly, The U.S. Patent and Trademark Office reported awarding about 300,000 patents per year, thereby implying the immense potential in patenting unique inventions alone.

Lastly, providing online consultancy services masks the geographical barriers and extends one's reach to a wider global audience. It also offers convenience, flexibility and personal brand development. As noted by Forrester Research, the online consultation market is expected to grow to $16 billion by 2025.

Undeniably, these career options emanate independence, job satisfaction, and promising financial returns. Embracing them doesn't necessarily mean forgoing other income sources but rather diversifying one's income stream, thereby cultivating an additional layer of financial security. In conclusion, novel career solutions, driven by innovation and creativity, exemplify the transformative potential in our evolving professional environment. By aligning our unique talents with market needs, we can script our financial destiny and stride ahead with an audacious spirit of entrepreneurship.

Let's take the example of Rob Percival, a former mathematics teacher from Cambridge, England. Unsatisfied with the traditional job system and the constraints it imposed, Rob dived into the world of digital entrepreneurship and passive income. He created a series of coding courses and launched them online on Udemy, a well-known online learning platform.

His courses, comprehensively titled 'The Complete Web Development Course', quickly filled a niche in the e-learning market - helping beginners grasp complex programming concepts in an easy-to-understand manner. The series became wildly popular, drawing over 1.2 million students from all over the globe, subsequently, contributing to a share of Udemy's $200 million revenue in 2019, as reported by Forbes.

What set Rob's course apart from many others, was the novelty of his teaching methods, such as incorporating project-based learning, ensuring students could practice new skills on real projects, which subsequently solved the problem of students having theoretical knowledge with no practical experience. Additionally, he updated his course with new content, ensuring it stayed relevant and useful - directly addressing the problem of outdated material in the fast-paced world of web development.

This venture not only made Rob financially independent but also enabled him to establish Codestars, a successful e-learning company with several instructors. His story illustrates how creatively leveraging skills and knowledge can bear fruitful results in the digital era.

Finding a good solution to a problem radiates positive impacts throughout every dimension of a person's life. On the emotional front, removing the weight of a troubling issue typically reduces feelings of stress and anxiety, ushering in a sense of peace and satisfaction. The mental strain we often associate with ongoing problems eases, bolstering self-esteem and leading to renewed confidence in one's abilities to overcome obstacles. Over time, this serves to strengthen problem-solving capabilities and offers a more resilient perspective on adversity.

If the issue at hand was causing direct or indirect physical distress - an ailment, or perhaps stress-induced symptoms - its resolution can have a simultaneously palpable and profound impact on one's physical health. Similarly, when problems entangled with finances are solved, it can lead to improved financial stability. The simple act of curtailing unnecessary expenditure or improving one's earning potential can encourage growth and open up fresh saving opportunities.

In terms of our social interactions, any conflict or discord that was previously causing tension can be smoothed out, leading to healthier, more fulfilling relationships. Not only does this enrich personal life, but it impartially extends into the professional realm too. Solving problems at work can lead to an uptick in job satisfaction, pave the way for career advancement, and propel overall professional growth.

Lastly, there's a lesser-spoken, somewhat subtle dimension impacted when we solve issues - our spiritual well-being. Resolving problems can offer a deep sense of inner peace, an increased self-awareness leading to personal growth. Altogether, finding a solution to a problem weaves a complex tapestry of interrelated benefits across every area of our lives, leading to holistic growth and well-being.

In conclusion, the exploration of innovative career solutions, such as passive income and solopreneurship, has proven that they serve as a robust conduit to achieving financial and professional fulfillment. Whether it's creating digital products that can be perpetually monetized, delving into the realm of virtual real estate, monetizing intellectual property, or leveraging one's expertise to provide online consultancy services, these solutions clearly usher a new era of work. Tapping into these frontier strategies requires not only the courage to tread unfamiliar terrains but also inspired creativity and unique skills. Yet, the outcomes hold great promise. Shattering the norms of traditional 9-to-5 jobs, these solutions introduce a work-life balance that matches both financial and personal needs. They offer an unprecedented sense of autonomy and an opportunity to ride the swift wave of digital evolution, right at the heart of the future of work. Importantly, they also epitomize the diversification of income streams, an aspect critical to modern financial security. Even though the journey may involve challenges and demands a shift in mindset, these rewarding solutions are potent enough to redefine our professional trajectories and carve out a path for long-lasting success. As we stand at the threshold of these transformative times, with open minds and audacious spirits, it is ripe for us to take the leap and explore the exhilarating horizon of innovative career solutions.

CHAPTER 5: EMBRACING THE DHARMA OF FINANCIAL INDEPENDENCE

Fear and desire often limit our ambitions. To break down that limitation, we must engage with spiritual effort. Seeking wealth isn't an unfounded desire but an opportunity to serve the world and find your true potential, Ahjan Samvara.

Money, most of us have been conditioned to believe, is the root of all evil, a belief that convolutes our relationship with it. Yet, what if we shift our perspective and reframe money as a mere energy or tool that echoes our intentions?

As a spiritual practitioner, you might feel guilty for aspiring financial independence or passive income. As students of spirituality, we're often conflicted with the norms of the monastic vow of poverty. However, as a Buddhist monk and a lineage teacher, I'm here to tell you that your aspiration for financial freedom is not only permissible but also worthwhile.

Passive income, in essence, is money earned with minimal activity through a variety of ventures which require a significant upfront monetary or time investment. This could be from real-estate rentals, a blog, an online course, or even investing in a startup. In a way, you invest upfront in the form of time, energy and resources, to reap the benefits in due course without active involvement - the very essence of the law of karma.

In life, our primary goal is not just to survive but to flourish. Financial independence fetches us the freedom to contribute to society and follow our spiritual pursuits without the constant worry of making ends meet. What we can learn from the Zen practice of mindfulness is that it inherently asks us to be financially mindful as well. Establishing a healthy relationship with money is as crucial as establishing a healthy meditation practice.

When we view financial independence from the lens of Buddhist teachings, it aligns with the principle of Right Livelihood. This underpins the idea that our professional life should not only support our living but should also contribute positively to our community. This mutual benefit amplifies our Bodhisattva vow - the aspiration to achieve Buddhahood for the benefit of all sentient beings.

Initially, it might seem like the pursuit of passive income and a dedicated spiritual practice are conflicting goals. But in reality, when navigated mindfully and ethically, they can complement each other. The essence of the spiritual teachings and the pursuit of passive income share a common base - they both require us to be forward-thinking, patient and resilient.

In a more practical sense, the stability and autonomy that come with financial freedom can contribute to deepening your spiritual practices. The less time and energy you spend worrying about your next paycheck, the more you have to devote to your personal and spiritual growth.

Thus, the spiritual solution for generating passive income and achieving financial freedom is rooted in mindfulness and Right Livelihood. Develop the skills necessary to generate sources of passive income. While doing so, ensure that your ventures align with your principles and contribute positively to society. This will not solely benefit you financially but will also amplify your spiritual growth and fulfillment.

Remember, passive income is not about reaping benefits with minimal effort but about mindfully making an upfront investment. Like any spiritual quest, it also requires dedication, patience, resilience and above all ethicality. Embrace this notion of balance between spiritual and financial wellness and you will find yourself truly enriched.

In the words of Lao Tzu, Be content with what you have; rejoice in the way things are. When you realize there is nothing lacking, the whole world belongs to you. So, do not just seek financial freedom. Seek balance, seek harmony and, most importantly, seek understanding of self and the world around you. That is the true path to freedom.

The spiritual pursuit for financial freedom and passive income may seem overwhelming. Still, when navigated mindfully, it can be an enlightening journey that complements your spiritual journey. Here are some key insights rooted in Buddhist teachings that can guide you towards this path.

Start by reframing your understanding of wealth. In Buddhism, wealth is not seen as inherently good or evil but as an instrument that reflects the intentions of the person wielding it. If approached with greed or attachment, wealth could serve as a barrier to spiritual growth. Yet, if approached with mindfulness and compassion, wealth can be a tool to sustain oneself and others, allowing one to devote more time and energy to spiritual growth.

Right Livelihood, part of the Buddha's Noble Eightfold Path, is a principle that guides us towards work that not only supports our material needs but also contributes positively to our community. When viewed in the framework of this principle, the pursuit of passive income is not inherently opposed to Buddhist teachings. It's instead about creating a venture that brings about mutual prosperity.

Engage in your work as a form of meditation. Like meditation, work involves discipline, focus, and wisdom. When you perform your work with mindfulness, integrity, and dedication, the boundaries between your spiritual and professional lives are dissolved.

Maintaining an attitude of service is crucial. When seeking ways to generate passive income, ask yourself, What problems can I solve?

How can I serve others? By aligning your financial pursuits with the selfless intent of service, work can become an extension of your spiritual path.

Remember to disentangle your self-worth from your net-worth. Your wealth or lack thereof does not define your worth or spiritual prowess. Do not let the pursuit of passive income lead you towards attachment or aversion, two of the central causes of suffering in Buddhism. Instead, develop a balanced perspective towards money, viewing it as a tool rather than a measure of success.

Add a sprinkle of patience and persistence. The Buddhist practice of patience, or khanti, is a powerful force that helps us maintain a calm and accepting mind even in the face of life's difficulties. Most passive income ventures won't be immediately successful - they require time, dedication, and adaptability. So, like your spiritual journey, be patient and persistent.

Lastly, remember the impermanence of all things. In Buddhism, the understanding that everything is subject to change is fundamental. Money comes and goes, markets rise and fall, but your ability to maintain inner peace and stability amidst these exterior fluctuations is your greatest asset on both your spiritual and financial journeys.

In essence, the spiritual solution for passive income and financial freedom is rooted in Right Livelihood, mindfulness, service, balance, patience, and understanding impermanence. It's about transforming the pursuit of passive income into a path of spiritual and ethical growth. By integrating these spiritual principles into your financial endeavors, you can cultivate an enriching life, abundant in both material and spiritual wealth.

As a Buddhist teacher, I am well aware of the seemingly contradictory notions of seeking financial abundance and pursuing spiritual liberation. However, navigating these waters need not be a turbulent journey. As you have already understood, wealth is but an instrument and the value it holds is bestowed upon by the one who wields it. Now, let's delve deeper into how one can be rich in both material wealth and spiritual growth.

Selfless action is a significant aspect of the Buddhist teachings. The term for this in Sanskrit is 'Karma Yoga', the yoga of action. Taking this stance in your passive income ventures, by focusing on how your efforts are contributing to the betterment of others, can dovetail your financial pursuits with your spiritual practices.

Patience is not only about waiting; it is about maintaining a good attitude while waiting. Building a passive income stream is often a game of patience. It requires a calm and composed mind to persist when results aren't immediate. These moments of waiting can be an opportunity for spiritual growth, a chance for you to practice calmness and equanimity.

There's also the factor of managing your financial resources wisely. In the Anguttara Nikaya, Buddha talks about the wisdom of saving and investing money. He advises his followers to divide their wealth into four parts - one for enjoyment, two for daily business, and one for emergency situations. Parallelly, we can apply the principle of balance in our quest for passive income, ensuring that our resources are allocated wisely and that we are securing our financial future without compromising on our present happiness.

In the discourse of Sukha Sutta, Buddha elaborates on happiness. He emphasizes the happiness arising from debtlessness and the happiness arising from saving. As you venture into generating passive income, it's crucial to not just focus on revenue generation but also on managing your existing wealth. Ensuring that you live a content life unburdened by debts can contribute significantly to your sense of happiness and peace.

In terms of embracing passive sources of income, we must guard against the vice of sloth. The Dhammapada contains Buddha's dire warnings against laziness. Despite the term passive, creating streams of passive income requires active effort, at least in the initial stages. Therefore, approaching this with diligence becomes vital.

Truly embracing the dharma of financial independence means acknowledging both your own needs and the needs of others. It involves holding space for your aspirations while also crafting a vision that adds value to the world. It is about giving and receiving in a balanced, harmonious manner. Therefore, balance between your worldly pursuits and your spiritual advancement isn't just possible but a sustainable and harmonious way to live a rich and rewarding life.

The prevailing mindset in our society, influenced by consumerism and materialism, often equates wealth and possessions directly with happiness and fulfilment. The pursuit of wealth is viewed as an absolute good, regardless of the circumstances or the methods used. This fixation with material wealth leads to a never-ending rat race, resulting in stress, anxiety, and a consistent feeling of dissatisfaction.

Research reinforces this stance. For instance, a study by Princeton University's Woodrow Wilson School found that after reaching an income of about $75,000 per year, people's day-to-day happiness does not increase significantly with additional income. It suggests that above a certain financial comfort level, more money does not lead to more happiness.

Another research published in the Proceedings of the National Academy of Sciences found that individuals who prioritized time over money reported greater happiness. The overemphasis on wealth accumulation invariably leads to compromised personal time and resultant dissatisfaction.

In stark contrast, Buddhism emphasizes inner peace and personal contentment. It views wealth, not as an end in itself, but merely as a means to an end. Wealth can provide basic comforts and fulfill material needs, but it holds little promise in providing genuine fulfilment or peace of mind. Buddha advocated for moderation, the 'Middle Way', shunning both indulgence in sensual pleasures and the practice of severe asceticism.

Buddhism also stresses the impermanent nature of material wealth. Possessions can be lost, stolen, or destroyed; money can be spent or devalued. Therefore, equating such transient entities with lasting happiness is a recipe for disappointment.

On the other hand, inner peace and spiritual development, which Buddhism promotes, are non-material entities that are not subject to theft, loss, or devaluation. They are timeless and enduring, providing an unshakeable foundation for deep-seated contentment and happiness.

The relentless pursuit of wealth for its own sake, to the detriment of personal time and peace of mind, is clearly an unhealthy approach that brings about limited rewards. Fostering a mindset that places equal importance on spiritual growth alongside generating income can support a balanced, fulfilling life. Such a holistic approach is not only beneficial for one's peace of mind, but also, as Buddhist teachings advocate, helps in making better decisions, nurturing healthier relationships, and supporting the wellness of the wider community.

Let's embark on a journey of truth and transformation. Our starting point is the whirlpool of conceptually conflicting desires - the yearning for spiritual liberation and the pursuit of financial prosperity. Within this dichotomy, paradoxically, lies the path to harmony.

The realm of finance is not innately at odds with Buddhism but can be transmuted into a spiritual quest itself. Remember, as we embark, this journey demands both a sailor's dexterity and a pirate's spirit— navigation and audacity, patience and perseverance with a dash of daring when required.

Picture, if you will, a mighty river, a body of life-giving water coursing across terrains. It changes as it flows - sometimes placid, sometimes raging, but always unhindered. This river is a reflection of your financial pursuit. At times, it requires active effort, at other times, passivity is key, but it should always be rooted in firm principles.

Visualize this journey as an enactment of the Sanskrit concept of 'Karma Yoga' - the yoga of selfless action. This principle is akin to converting worldly business into a compassionate venture. The focus is less on increasing material wealth for personal gain, and more on creating prosperity that trickles down and enriches others.

Now imagine a lighthouse guiding ships amidst the raging tempest. This beacon symbolizes the virtue of wisdom. Drawing from the words of Buddha from the Anguttara Nikaya, structuring your financial sphere wisely equates to having such a beacon in your journey. The key lies in a judicious attitude towards your resources, propelling increased savings and sound investments without denying yourself goodly experiences of life.

The notion of patience is comparable to the oars steering the boat across the river. Building a passive income stream is often a test of patience and persistence. These periods offer a window of opportunity for self-growth, allowing you to cultivate calmness, composure, and equanimity.

Debtlessness and saving, as Buddha named the sources of happiness in the Sukha Sutta, are the strongholds you build along this river. Prioritize not just augmenting revenue, but organizing existing wealth. The act of clearing debt can stimulate an unburdened existence, propelling a sense of inner fulfillment.

Now, visualize the mighty river turning into a majestic waterfall. This transformation embodies the transition from active to passive income generation. It crystallizes the necessity of not mistaking the term passive for idleness. Instead, it is a call for diligent effort, especially in the initial stages.

As your financial voyage aligns itself with Buddhist teachings, the striking reality unfolds. The quest for financial freedom becomes an exquisite dance with life, intertwining personal aspirations and ethical values. This balanced co-existence engenders financial stability without forsaking spiritual profundity.

Thus, this journey reveals how Buddhism's timeless wisdom can weave itself seamlessly into your pursuit of financial independence. And this process, my friend, is not a detour from your spiritual path but an enriching part of the path itself.

Let yourself be swept into this sophisticated dance of life, where spiritual fortification meets financial mastery. Embrace the adventure. May your journey be a testament to the harmonious integration of spiritual and material prosperity, nurturing joy and spiritual growth in you and others alike.

Navigating this path involves understanding the underpinnings of your financial predicaments and tracing them to their very roots - your mindsets, views, and perceptions about money, and yourself. Herein lies the key - the problem is not money itself, but your relationship with it.

Frequently, we are entangled in financial issues, not because of a factual lack of resources, but because of our perspectives towards wealth and self-worth. It's like gazing at a distorted reflection. What you perceive is tainted by the ripples of emotionally loaded assumptions and evaluations about wealth and abundance.

As we march forward on this expedition, shedding these distortive views becomes vital. You're not just untangling the external complications of financial management, but unraveling profound layers of internal self-awareness. It's a two-pronged approach that brings transformation both in the tangible world of finance and the intangible arena of the mind.

To leverage this emotionally neutral perspective towards wealth, we anchor ourselves to the teachings of 'Right Understanding' embedded in the Buddhist Eightfold Path. By nurturing a Right Understanding, we disassociate our self-value from our net worth, thus countering one of the sources of our financial woes.

The practice of 'Right Intent,' another aspect of the Eightfold Path, invites ethical intention into your financial pursuits. This ethical compass inherently aligns your fiscal goals to the higher principles of compassion and kindness. Gradually, wealth acquisition and financial success become an act of service - service to oneself and others.

By adopting these principles, we tap into the potential to reconstruct our financial destiny, transforming it from a source of stress into a wellspring of stability and serenity. It helps you strive towards prosperity without straying from spiritual tenets, thereby unraveling a solution to the battle between moral integrity and material growth.

Hence, the root of financial success in the Buddhist framework lies not in mere wealth accumulation, but in building a holistic paradigm of prosperity that integrates spiritual growth with financial development.

By illuminating how the teachings of the Buddha lay a foundation for sound wealth building and management principles, you align yourself with a way of living that cultivates not just financial freedom but spiritual enlightenment.

Remember, the journey to financial independence in Buddhism is not merely an external endeavour reacting to market conditions or economic trends. It is an inner journey, a process of self-realization. As your perception towards wealth realigns, it influences your external financial behaviour. Thus, the solution to financial dilemmas lies less in figuring out the complex world outside and more in deciphering and mastering the world within.

Embracing this novel perspective based on Buddhist principles can yield profound advantages that are both transformative and pragmatic. Let's explore how this integration of spiritual and financial arenas can lead to personal and societal betterment.

Firstly, the personal growth that accompanies this novel approach is immeasurable. The promise of financial freedom is compelling in itself, but coupled with spiritual growth, it transforms into an even more captivating prospect. By aligning financial pursuits with Buddhist principles, you impart a spiritual undertone to even the most practical of actions. This combination allows for unprecedented personal evolution, helping individuals develop a more profound understanding of their finances, their spiritual path and how the two intertwine.

Moreover, the Buddhist philosophy of selflessness inherently promotes the principle of financial giving as a means for personal fulfillment and societal good. By reconfiguring our traditional perceptions of wealth, we open ourselves up to the joy and satisfaction that comes from leveraging our financial prosperity for the welfare of all. Such an approach encourages a shift from a self-centered attitude to a community-centric viewpoint. This philosophy could potentially contribute to alleviating socioeconomic disparities and forge a society rooted in compassion and shared prosperity.

Further, viewing wealth management through a Buddhist lens can lead to improved mental health. Money-related stressors, stemming from the scarcity mindset or debt burdens, are rampant in modern society. However, by applying the principles of the Eightfold Path to finances—especially those related to Right Understanding and Right Intent—individuals can cultivate a healthier relationship with money. Such a perspective can diffuse the stress commonly associated with money, fostering a peaceful mind and a more balanced life.

Studies in the field of neurofinance reinforce this view, suggesting a direct correlation between our cognitive-emotional responses and financial behaviors. Thus, by transforming our attitudes and emotions towards money, we can effectively change our financial behaviors. This shift can catalyze better financial decisions, promoting growth and stability.

Furthermore, behavioural economists like Richard Thaler champion the idea of 'mental accounting'—how people categorize and treat money. Viewing money management as an aspect of spiritual practice can inspire positive mental accounting strategies, fostering well-being and abundance.

Lastly, the ability to infuse spirituality into mundane financial dealings can also impact broader spheres, including business and economy. Imagine corporations with not just financial goals but ethical and spiritual ones too. This approach could redefine success, highlighting the importance of corporate responsibility and sustainable practices.

In essence, the integration of finance and spirituality as illuminated by Buddhism presents the potential for transformative personal, societal, and even global change. An individual's approach to financial matters becomes ennobled, going beyond mere personal gain. A society becomes more equitable, underpinned by the shared responsibility of wealth distribution. And a world stands to gain, guided by the ethical, responsible, and sustainable handling of wealth – a beacon in turbulent financial times. Such an approach holds the promise of a future where financial freedom is the norm, not the exception, and it is reached not at the expense of others but in harmony with all.

Consider the example of Mark, a hardworking entrepreneur who started his own technology company. His business thrived, brought innovative solutions and created lucrative job opportunities. However, with increasing financial success, Mark noticed a growing sense of unease and dissatisfaction within himself. He began to question the actual worth of his wealth and the relentless pursuit of financial growth. This led to stress, anxiety and a growing sense of disconnection from his own life and values.

During a sabbatical, Mark encountered Buddhist teachings and started to see his circumstances from a fresh perspective. He learned about the Eightfold Path and began to apply the principle of 'Right Understanding' to his relationship with wealth. He started to recognize that his discomfort didn't stem from his wealth itself, but from his attachment to it, and the fear of losing it. This insight was transformative for Mark, as he began to disentangle his sense of self-worth from his financial worth.

Next, he sought to integrate the Buddhist principle of 'Right Intent' into his business. He redefined his profit objectives to align with an ethical approach, focusing on fairness, equitable wealth distribution and sustainable practices. He openly communicated his new vision to his team and encouraged them to integrate these values into their work.

Mark found that despite these shifts, his company continued to thrive financially, but the work environment was noticeably more fulfilling and harmonious. Some even found that their productivity and creativity improved as they were motivated by a purpose greater than just profits.

Moreover, Mark redirected a portion of the company's profits towards community development projects, thereby offering his wealth back to society. This practice of generosity added a new dimension to his perception of wealth as he realized the joy and inner richness that accompanies giving.

Mark's overall quality of life improved remarkably. He noticed a significant reduction in his stress levels and anxiety, his relationships were more stable, and he experienced a sense of inner peace and contentment, something he had not felt when his focus was solely on financial growth.

Mark's story illustrates how Buddhist teachings can offer solutions to modern economic and personal challenges. Integrating these principles into your financial life can not only help accumulate wealth but also create a deeper sense of satisfaction, spiritual growth, and a profound understanding of one's relationship with money. The incorporation of spiritual practices into one's financial conduct begets manifold benefits, spanning several domains of life.

On a personal level, this integration fosters a healthier relationship with money. Instead of merely focusing on wealth accumulation, individuals begin to appreciate their financial resources from a standpoint of gratitude and respect. Such a perspective dispels the common fear and anxiety associated with money. Instead, there's an onset of clarity and calm, resulting in better decision-making.

In the social sphere, the principles of fairness, equanimity and compassion that underpin Buddhism can encourage more ethical and responsible financial behaviours. The practice of giving highlights the joy of sharing wealth, nurturing empathy, and fostering connections with others. This can consequently lead to a more harmonious and equitable society.

From a health perspective, this approach can significantly alleviate stress and anxiety associated with financial concerns. The practice of mindfulness aids in maintaining emotional balance, eliminating the typical stress triggers in our financial lives. Moreover, by keeping a non-attachment view towards wealth, individuals are less prone to the emotional turbulences characterised by swings in financial market dynamics.

Professionally, incorporating Buddhist principles into business practices leads to more ethical, fair, and sustainable decision-making. It promotes a win-win situation where businesses can still be profitable, while also contributing positively to society and the environment.

Finally, on the spiritual front, the intertwining of Buddhism and financial practice deepens one's spiritual journey. The application of the Eightfold Path to our financial lives acts as a continuous spiritual exercise, promoting spiritual growth and understanding. The inherent focus on ethics, mindfulness, and wisdom in our financial decisions aligns with the nourishment of our spiritual being.

In sum, the fusion of financial management with Buddhist practices benefits all aspects of an individual's life, creating a more balanced, ethical, and spiritually enriched lifestyle.
In conclusion, integrating Buddhist spirituality with our financial actions and decisions generates deep-seated positive transformations. It significantly reduces financial stress and anxiety by cultivating a healthier relationship with money. By seeing money as a tool, instead of a source of happiness or security, our fears and anxieties surrounding it dissipate. Instead, we operate from a space of calm clarity and conscious decision-making.

Furthermore, Buddhist principles foster ethical financial behaviours, promoting fairness, equanimity, and compassion. The act of giving and sharing cultivates a sense of connection and empathy, contributing to social harmony and equity. In the professional sphere, businesses guided by these principles engage in more responsible, fair and sustainable practices, creating a win-win situation for all stakeholders involved.

Ultimately, the infusion of Buddhist practices into our financial lives forms a constant spiritual exercise, facilitating spiritual growth and deepening our understanding of life. This approach helps create a more balanced, ethical, and spiritually enriched life. It assists us in navigating the vast and complex world of finance with wisdom and ease, benefitting not only ourselves but also our communities, society and the environment at large.

Embracing the dance of spirituality and finance thus lights our path towards a more purposeful, harmonious and contented existence.

Title: The Triad of Passive Income Solutions: Embracing Mind, Career, and Spirituality

Embarking on the journey towards financial freedom through passive income requires understanding and integrating three unique solutions into your lifestyle.

The mind-blowing solution focuses on innovative financial strategies to diversify investments and maximize potential returns. Real estate, smartphone apps, e-commerce, and cryptocurrency are key areas to explore in the search for low-input high-yield investments.

On the other hand, the career solution suggests gaining financial independence through mastery of passive income generation, requiring thorough planning, resilience, and resource optimization. This strategy involves transitioning from traditional methods towards more innovative ways of income generation that do not necessarily require your constant involvement or effort.

Finally, the spiritual solution is about acknowledging and aligning your financial pursuits with your spiritual path. Couched in Buddhist teachings, this solution emphasizes the mindfulness approach to managing wealth and creating shared prosperity through serving others. Cultivating patience and persistence and recognising the impermanence of everything, including financial situations, are also valuable perspectives when pursuing passive income.

In conclusion, the key to unlocking passive income lies in balancing innovative investment strategies, career planning and leveraging spiritual principles. When these methods are combined effectively, they can facilitate sustainable financial freedom.

Imagine an individual, let's call her Lisa. She is a successful software engineer, with her career peaking. Despite her success, Lisa yearns for more flexibility and freedom to spend time on her passions and with her loved ones. She decides to tap into her skill set and develop a mindfulness app to guide users through meditation and other relaxation techniques.

Firstly, Lisa employs her tech-savvy nature and her understanding of the mind-blowing solution. She invests her time and resources into creating an app with a unique selling proposition - integrating technology with spiritual science for stress reduction. She uses her knowledge to provide a seamless user experience.

Her next step is to develop a business model that provides passive income. She sets up a subscription-based model for the app, where users pay a small monthly fee for access to premium content and features. This is where the career solution comes into play. Lisa is leveraging her expertise in software engineering and her understanding of business strategies to create a sustainable income stream.

For Lisa, her app isn't just about making money, it's a labor of love and a way she can share the benefits of mindfulness with others. Inculcating her spiritual solution, Lisa pours her heart into ensuring that every aspect of the app fosters peace, tranquillity, and a sense of balance.

As her app gains popularity, she expands into offering branded merchandise, another avenue for passive income. She partners with ethical manufacturing companies, ensuring that her business aligns with her spiritual and ethical values.

This example combines the power of the mind-blowing solution, through mindful use of technology and investment in app creation; the career solution, through building a sustainable business model; and the spiritual solution, through aligning it all with a genuine drive to enhance mental well-being. It also brings to the table an innovative way to generate a passive income, through branded merchandise.

The benefits of this approach are profound. On a personal level, Lisa succeeds in transitioning from an active income, where she was trading her time for money, to a passive income, giving her the freedom she craved. Emotionally and spiritually, Lisa's contentment and satisfaction levels rise, knowing that she is positively impacting people's lives. Her financial stability improves and becomes more in line with her psychological well-being. She is successful in creating a balanced life for herself, which incorporates financial success, spirituality, and a feeling of meaningful contribution. Such personal fulfillment and satisfaction can't be quantified, and reflect a state of true prosperity.

The optimal solution in this case is a combination of a mind-blowing, career, and spiritual solution. This combination entails utilizing one's unique skills, in this case technology and application development, to create a product that not only serves others but also aligns with personal interests and spiritual beliefs. This solution also incorporates a smart business model that secures a continuous stream of income.

This triumvirate approach offers numerous benefits. Firstly, it allows for the pursuit of personal passions through an engaging and meaningful project. Secondly, it offers financial stability through a passive income stream. Finally, it delivers personal fulfillment as you're contributing positively to the lives of others.

In the following sections of this book, we will delve into this combined solution in greater depth. We will walk you through each step of using your unique skills and spiritual interests to create a product, develop an effective business model, and ultimately achieve personal and financial fulfillment. The journey to prosperity is often complex, but with the right guidance, it can be an enlightening and rewarding experience.

Empowered Pathways: Curating Success on Your Own Terms

As we draw this chapter to a close, dear reader, we want to acknowledge the courage and openness it requires to embark on a journey towards transforming oneself, and by extension, one's reality. What lies ahead is not a one-size-fits-all solution, but a tailor-made blueprint for success that rises from the confluence of your unique skill sets, aspirations, and sublime life purposes.

Just envision the immense universe of possibilities that await you. Imagine developing and launching that app, creating that course or product, living a life fueled by passion and supported by a steady stream of passive income. Picture the awed faces of your friends and family as they marvel at your achievements, the smiles of satisfaction on the faces of your satisfied customers, and, most importantly, the deep well of joy in your heart, knowing that you're living life fully, passionately, and on your own terms.

The next chapter, 'Action Plan,' is not merely a set of instructions but a journey of self-discovery. It will guide you within, into the depths of your potential and outwards into the world of endless manifestations. It will set you upon a path where every step taken is a mark of progress, of growth, and ultimately, a mark of your success.

Preparing for this journey may seem daunting at first, but remember, dear reader, as Rumi once said, "The only step that matters is the next one." All great journeys in life begin with one small step, taken with faith and steadfast determination.

So, as you move ahead, remember to breathe, to cherish the journey, and most importantly, to believe in yourself. You are capable, you are worthy, and you are powerful beyond measure. You are about to prove it to yourself, to mold your life into a masterpiece of your own making.

You will wake up each day with enthusiasm and retire each night with satisfaction, knowing that you are living a life designed by you, and not dictated by circumstances. Picture this in vivid detail; breathe life into your visualizations and let this richness of detail power your leap into action.

The path towards success in life is not always easy, but it is worthwhile. The upcoming chapter will guide you through an effective, personalized action plan that honors your individuality, nurtures your spiritual alignment, and propels you towards a fulfilling life shrouded in prosperity. This snapshot of the art of living fully, passionately, and successfully is within your reach. So, brace yourself to embrace it.

Remember, this is no ordinary book. This is a transformative journey. A journey towards curating success on your own terms. Now, let's take that journey together. Let's commence your ascend towards a passionate, prosperous, and fulfilling life. Turn the page, and let's get started with the 'Action Plan.' The future that you've always dreamed about awaits you with open arms. It's time to make that dream your reality.

CHAPTER 6: EMBARKING ON THE POSITIVE MINDSET JOURNEY: A GATEWAY TO PASSIVE INCOME AND FINANCIAL FREEDOM.

If one desires financial freedom through passive income, two main factors must be initially considered: mindset, which lays the foundation for success, and the technical details about passive income generation methods. This discussion primarily focuses on the power of the positive mindset and how this mental state plays a pivotal role in achieving financial freedom.

The concept of a positive mindset revolves around the belief of seeing the world through a lens of optimism and opportunities rather than pessimism and obstacles. A positive mindset is the ability to have a proactive, optimistic, and resilient attitude. It involves a willingness to push through tough circumstances, to learn continuously, and to keep persevering, armed with the belief that success is within reach.

When it comes to achieving financial freedom via passive income, a positive mindset allows an individual to better manage the associated risks and challenges. Passive income often involves considerable upfront effort, such as researching, planning, and perhaps making initial investments. As such, many people get discouraged at this stage. However, individuals equipped with a positive mindset perceive these initial tasks as stepping stones to their success. They embrace the effort and potential challenges, understanding that the initial hard work will pave the way for future ease and financial growth.

Adopting a positive mindset fosters creativity and resourcefulness, two characteristics essential in creating and sustaining passive income. A person with a positive mindset tends to see possibilities instead of hurdles. Off the beaten track ideas start to seem achievable, their mind becomes fertile ground for innovative passive income strategies, and they remain motivated to actualize their financial dreams.

Moreover, resilience is another significant component of a positive mindset crucial in the realm of passive income. Given that passive income often involves certain risks and uncertainties, it's inevitable to encounter setbacks and failures along the journey. However, individuals with a positive mindset use failures as learning opportunities. They bounce back quickly, adjust their strategies following setbacks, and remain tenacious on their path towards financial freedom.

Lastly, a positive mindset dovetails directly with the very essence of passive income — freedom, flexibility, and the luxury to enjoy life while the money keeps flowing in. Since people with a positive mindset are often less stressed, more opportunistic, and overall happier, they are more likely to make sound investment decisions and persist until they attain their financial independence goals.

In essence, the value of a positive mindset when pursuing a passive income — and thus financial freedom — is immeasurable. This mental resilience enables tenacity during challenging times, creativity in developing income syreams, and an overall happier, healthier life that aligns perfectly with the ultimate objectives of earning a passive income. Therefore, adopting a positive mindset is the first step to embark on the path of financial freedom through passive income.

Creating a positive mindset is nothing short of a magical process. The fact that you have control over your thoughts and emotions which, in turn, can fashion your experiences and mold your life, is an absolutely empowering concept.

Positive thinking is a gem in the crown of a positive mindset. It is where you actively make a conscious effort to view situations, events, and circumstances in a positive light. It involves an adjustment of perspective, where you identify the silver lining or the beneficial aspects of an otherwise gloomy scenario. Positive thinking does not mean that you ignore the negatives. Instead, it promotes an optimistic outlook where you embrace both successes and failures as part of the learning process. This mindset can have profound impacts on your everyday life including better stress management, improved health, and a greater level of happiness and satisfaction.

Overcoming fear is an integral part of fostering a positive mentality. Fear is a common human emotion which, if left unchecked, can paralyze you and halt your forward progress. Learning to overcome fear involves recognizing that fear is a natural and normal part of life, and that it can, in fact, be a catalyst for growth. Once you realize this, you can begin to deconstruct your fear, understanding its roots, its triggers, and how it manifests in your life. Slowly but surely, you can then replace your fear-based thoughts with positive affirmations, allowing you to move from a state of fear to a state of courage and initiative.

Closely connected to overcoming fear is the concept of overcoming doubt. Self-doubt can keep you trapped in a cycle of insecurity and inhibit your growth. Overcoming self-doubt requires you to identify and challenge any negative self-talk that sows seeds of doubt in your mind. It involves developing an attitude of self-compassion and understanding, focusing on your strengths rather than your imperfections, and interpreting failures not as evidence of incapacity, but as opportunities for growth and learning.

Believing in yourself ties into the theme of overcoming doubt. It is about having confidence in your abilities and recognizing that you are capable of achieving your goals. This belief will inspire you to take action and persist in the face of challenges. You start by acknowledging your successes, no matter how small they may seem, and using them to cement your belief in your capabilities. Each success will then fuel your self-belief and propel you forward.

Mediation is a powerful way to clear away negative thoughts and reset your mind for success. Meditation is stilling thoughts and centering yourself. Mediation is the cultivation of a clear, focused, and positive mindset. It helps you let go of limiting beliefs, to instill confidence, and visualize success.

Here are some benefits meditation offers for a positive financial mindset:

Clarity and Focus: Meditation clears the mental clutter, allowing you to focus on your financial goals and the steps needed to achieve them.

Reduces Stress: Financial concerns are a major source of stress for many. Meditation helps manage this stress, allowing for clearer thinking and better decision-making.

Reframes Relationship with Money: By addressing and releasing limiting beliefs, meditation can help in reshaping your relationship with money from one of fear or scarcity to one of abundance and opportunity.

Boosts Confidence: Visualization and positive affirmations enhance self-belief, empowering you to take calculated risks and make informed choices.

Enhances Decision-making: A calm and clear mind can assess situations better, leading to smarter, more informed financial decisions.

Fosters Gratitude: Recognizing and appreciating what you already have can lead to a more contented and abundant mindset.

Attracts Positivity: A positive mindset attracts positive outcomes. By regularly visualizing success, you align your actions and decisions towards achieving it.

Here is a ten minute daily practice:

Preparation: Find a calm, quiet space free from distractions. Sit comfortably with a straight back, either on a cushion, chair, or the floor. Close your eyes and take a few deep breaths.

Release Limiting Beliefs: Bring to mind any limiting beliefs you have about money or success. Common examples include "I don't deserve wealth" or "I can't make money". Visualize these beliefs as clouds. With each exhale, see them drift away, making space for positive affirmations.

Positive Affirmations: Start repeating positive affirmations either silently in your mind or out loud. Examples: "I am deserving of financial prosperity", "I am capable of making wise financial decisions", or "Every day, I am moving closer to my financial goals." Feel the weight and truth of these affirmations. Let them resonate deeply.

Visualization: Visualize yourself achieving your financial goals. See yourself confidently making decisions, experiencing financial growth, and enjoying the fruits of your success. Try to make this visualization as vivid as possible, involving all senses.

Gratitude: Think of what you already have, and feel a deep sense of gratitude. This step is crucial as it sets the tone for abundance and acknowledges the wealth you already possess.

Conclusion:

Sit in stillness focusing on the third eye, located between the eyebrows and slightly above. Sit in silence for as long as comfortable. Then slowly open your eyes and carry this positive, success-oriented energy with you throughout the day.

Mindfulness is a state of active, open attention to the present. It is about living in the moment and awakening to your current experiences, rather than dwelling in the past or anticipating the future. Mindfulness can help reduce stress, enhance performance, gain insight and awareness, and increase your attention to others' well-being. Mindfulness meditation in particular can help you cultivate this mindset, promoting a sense of calm and focus that can help you navigate through life's challenges with greater ease.

Visualization is a powerful mental practice used by many successful individuals. The basic concept is to imagine and visualize your goals as if you have already achieved them. This practice, relating highly to the law of attraction, allows your brain to practice to achieve success and moves you closer to your goals. You start by creating a detailed mental image of the desired outcome using all of your senses. Then, with regular practice, over time, your subconscious mind will begin to recognize this desired outcome as a part of your reality, making your goals seem more achievable.

In conclusion, cultivating a positive mindset involves positive thinking, overcoming fear and doubt, believing in yourself, being mindful, and using visualization. Embracing these elements in your journey will not only grant you a more vibrant and enjoyable life but also enhance your personal development leading you closer to overall success.

Be Positive: Think Your Way to Success

The fascinating journey to financial freedom using passive income targets not just the accumulation of wealth but also the improvement of mental resilience. Our mind, a fertile soil where both positive and negative thoughts mingle, plays a significant role in this endeavor. Your optimism and positivity can significantly accelerate this process. Here's a detailed guide on how you can use positive thinking to address passive income generation and gain financial freedom.

The first stride on this positivity path is the recognition of negative thoughts. It's an integral aspect as these negative thoughts often cloud our judgment, causing doubt and hindering progress. These could be fears of failure or doubts over the viability of your passive income streams. Identifying negative thoughts requires a reflective and contemplative approach. It involves self-awareness and understanding of your emotions, thought patterns, and reactions when dealing with financial matters.

Challenging these negative thoughts is the next step towards adopting a vibrant, positive thinking approach. It is essential not to suppress these thoughts but rather dispute them objectively. Ask yourself why you hold these beliefs. What experiences influenced your opinions? By contesting these negative thoughts and offering objective evidence against them, you disempower their hold over you. This process ultimately changes your mindset and makes room for positivity.

Having neutralized negativity, now it is time to introduce positive thoughts into your thought pool. It starts with a simple yet powerful intention to be positive. Make a conscious decision to approach every aspect of your life, most importantly, your journey to financial freedom, with positivity. This intentional positivity significantly reshapes your perspective towards passive income and bolsters your willingness to take necessary financial risks.

A fundamental part of cultivating positivity is to always look on the bright side of life, even in challenging situations. It's important to view hurdles not as setbacks but windows to growth. Troubles are not terminal, and the journey to financial freedom through passive income is not always seamless. These challenges are simply stepping stones, testing and strengthening your resilience and pushing you closer to your wealth goals.

Additionally, viewing problems as challenges to greatness greatly changes our reaction to these issues. Instead of seeing them as blockers, we visualize them as gateways to achieving a higher milestone. This fundamental shift in perspective aids in dissolving any form of negativity and replaces it with a powerful positivity that encourages a problem-solving mindset.

Finally, the use of affirmations, positive internal dialogue, considerably enhances one's positivity. Affirmations serve as reaffirming mantras that constantly remind you of your financial objectives and how much you can achieve. Feed your mind with affirmative statements about your financial progress. This powerful practice amplifies your self-belief and solidifies your positivity, ultimately boosting your chances of success in your quest for financial freedom through passive income.
Positive thinking, as its name suggests, is a mental and emotional attitude that revolves around a mindset of optimism and hopeful anticipation. It is not simply a relentless positivity or cheerful

demeanor, but a genuine belief in the value of opportunities, possibilities, and in one's own abilities. In the context of real-world practicality, it encourages solutions-orientated thinking, resilience in the face of adversity, and proactive choices that often lead to better health, increased productivity, less stress, and superior results in various life areas. It transforms challenges into opportunities and demands into privileges.

In the context of financial freedom with passive income, positive thinking plays a pivotal role. Passive income is any form of income that requires little to no effort to earn and maintain, usually coming from investments, royalties, real estate rentals, or business ventures that you are not actively involved in. Financial freedom, on the other hand, is the state of living without a dependency on employment income because your assets or passive income can adequately support your lifestyle expenses. The journey to this destination requires a substantial amount of discipline, diligence, conception of creative ideas, risk-taking, and patience; all of which are considerably fueled by positive thinking.

Now, let's illustrate this with a story - The Brave Investor.

Once upon a time, in a bustling city lived a man named Tom. Tom worked a 9 to 5 job, earning a decent salary, but he always dreamt of financial freedom. He had heard about passive income but had the common fear of failure discouraging him. His mindset began to shift after attending a seminar where he understood the significance of positive thinking. It's not about ignoring the risks, said the speaker, but about embracing the anticipation of success.

Motivated, Tom started studying various modes of passive income, reading books, listening to podcasts, and even attending seminars. He consciously replaced his fears with optimism, visualizing successful outcomes. Regardless of the challenges, Tom reflected positivity and resilience, adopting a solution-oriented approach. He looked at potential losses as a step closer to success rather than as failures.

He decided to invest in real estate, a venture famous for its potential to generate considerable passive income. Tom was aware it would take time, but he chose to remain patient, his positivity unwavering. He didn't let initial hiccups discourage him, analyzing them as learning points that enrich his investment journey.

Slowly but surely, Tom's investments started bearing fruits. The rentals from his properties generated enough income, steadily edging him towards his goal of financial freedom. Despite the hurdles along the way, his optimism, determination, and positive outlook carried him through, turning his dream of financial independence into a reality.

This tale highlights how positive thinking can be a catalyst in achieving real-world practical goals like financial freedom through passive income. It showcases that optimism not only fosters a happier mindset but also paves the way for actual, tangible success.

CHAPTER 7: UNEARTHING FINANCIAL FREEDOM: CONQUERING FEARS AND EMBRACING PASSIVE INCOME

The path towards financial freedom is often plagued by fear, hesitation, and doubt. Nevertheless, it's necessary to ascertain that these are but mere obstacles that can be overcome. To address fear concerning passive income and financial freedom, the methodology engages in meticulously filling the gaps in understanding, acquiring knowledge, asking for guidance, and practicing resilience.

Taking command of passive income can be intimidating, especially when you perceive it as a formidable, unexplored domain. Bridging the knowledge gap is essential, and this begins with comprehending the very essence of the phrase 'passive income'. Fundamentally, it refers to the earnings one acquires without actively being involved in a job or business. Once you are clear about what passive income is, the fear that stems from its unfamiliarity starts to wither.

The next step in overcoming fear involves acquiring knowledge. Investments, rentals, royalties, side businesses, are all prominent categories of passive income. Engaging deeply with each, learning how each works, and knowing the pros and cons can prove to be immensely effective in eradicating the fears attached to them. Equip yourself with knowledge both theoretical and practical and fear shall pave the way for confidence.

Guidance is a cornerstone in this journey of overcoming fear in your quest for financial freedom. A seasoned financial advisor, a friend who has experience with passive income, or perhaps a mentor can guide you along the arduous path. Being open to seeking advice and assistance can not only offer a fresh perspective but also bolster your faith in the potential of passive income.

Resilience, however, plays the most significant role in overcoming fear. The path to financial freedom is seldom linear. There will be setbacks and there will be failures. The value lies in not allowing these moments to claw into your apprehensions. Instead, interpret them as opportunities for growth and learning.

Here, it's noteworthy to stress the need to balance risk and caution in the pursuit of passive income for financial freedom. Never let the fear of striking out keep you from playing the game, but also ensure that you don't play blindly.

Notwithstanding the described fear-conquering methodology, remember the significance of being patient. Like any worthwhile pursuit, achieving financial freedom via passive income isn't instantaneous - it's a process, a journey. Frustration and fear might crop up every now and then, but continuing to walk the path with patience can lead you straight towards financial freedom.

Therefore, combating the fear associated with plunging into the world of passive income involves understanding the concept, arming oneself with knowledge, seeking guidance, remaining resilient, balancing risk and caution, and exercising patience. Liberation from the chains of fear promises to unlock the door to financial freedom.

Overcoming fear is a practical skill that involves understanding, confronting, and dealing with apprehension or worry in real-world scenarios. This might mean facing fears head-on or finding strategies to rationalize, minimize, or cope with the fear. Much like riding a bike or learning how to cook, it is a skill that can be learned, practiced, and mastered. In many areas of life, particularly when making substantial changes or taking notable risks, fear often jumps in, influencing our decisions and potentially steering us off our desired path. To gain control over fear, one typically employs a combination of mindfulness techniques, positive affirmations, and corrective reasoning.

Keeping this concept in mind, let's look at a real-world practical example that revolves around the theme of Passive Income for Financial Freedom:

In a small town lived a man named Anthony. He had a regular nine-to-five job and was content with his secure income. However, somewhere deep down, he had a gnawing fear of not having enough savings for his future, despite working tirelessly every day. This fear stopped him from exploring other opportunities or taking any investment risks.

One day, Anthony stumbled upon a seminar about passive income avenues. The idea of generating income without active intervention intrigued him. He learned about various passive income sources like rental properties, dividend stocks, blog or YouTube channel monetization, and affiliate marketing. It all sounded promising yet daunting.

After mulling it over, Anthony decided to face his fear and take the leap into the world of financial investments. He had a knack for storytelling and decided to start a blog, sharing tales from his travels and life experiences.

Anthony invested in learning about SEO and digital content marketing to grow his blog's reach. Overcoming his initial fear of loss, he also made small investments in dividend stocks with part of his savings. Slowly but steadily, his blog started gaining traction, and his ad revenues and stock dividends started bringing added income.

Months later, Anthony was not just a regular nine-to-five employee but a budding entrepreneur. Indeed, his transition had required work, but the income was now continuously flowing in irrespective of his active involvement—the very essence of passive income.

This tale of Anthony serves a real-world practical reminder that overcoming fear is the first step toward financial freedom. As an individual, Anthony has taken control of his financial future by introducing passive income streams and overcoming his fears, demonstrating that fear, while a daunting obstacle, can be confronted and mastered.

Title: Effortless Earnings: Embracing Passive Income for Financial Liberation

To address the concept of passive income for financial freedom, it is required to transcend the prevalent uncertainties that often surround this subject. This intricate process involves a few crucial steps that seek to assuage doubt and cultivate confidence in the feasibility of passive income as a viable route to financial liberty.

The first step is to enhance knowledge about passive income sources. Gaining extensive understanding about these income streams will aid in dispelling misconceptions. The caliber of this knowledge can be further enriched by comprehensive research about the effectiveness and efficiency of different passive income strategies such as rental income, affiliate marketing, and peer-to-peer lending amongst many others.

Parallel to garnering knowledge, it is essential to conceptualize a well-defined financial plan. Precise financial objectives and a systematic plan can significantly mitigate feelings of uncertainty. It aids in building a roadmap to achieve those goals, facilitating the transition from a regular income model to a more passive one. It's critical to bear in mind that while constructing a financial plan, it should be rooted in practicality and one's unique financial circumstances.

Simultaneously, tailoring the mindset is an ingredient for success in this financial journey. The art of patience is paramount in this context as passive income streams often require time to flourish.

Validating this fact can simultaneously help eliminate any remnants of unrealistic expectations that might stir up doubts and fears.

Embracing the concept of risk is another pivotal point in surmounting the barriers of doubt and fear. Recognizing that investing in passive income methods can host certain risks, and that all forms of investment inherently carry some degree of risk, can help to relieve the anxieties surrounding it. Instead of shying away from risk, learning to manage it effectively is the key to step forward with conviction.

Lastly, continual self-education proves instrumental in overcoming doubts. The economic landscape is dynamic, thus remaining updated about it and being open to modifications in our pre-established plans and strategies accordingly will assist in securing our financial future. Remember, knowledge diminishes fear.

In conclusion, overcoming doubt to embrace the idea of passive income for financial freedom revolves around a combination of in-depth knowledge, an organized plan, a tailored mindset, risk acceptance, and a lifelong learning commitment. The transformative course to financial freedom is not a sprint, but a marathon that tests and rewards patience, strategic thinking, and resilience.

CHAPTER 8: HARNESSING SELF-BELIEF AND PASSIVE INCOME FOR FINANCIAL LIBERTY

Believing in oneself, when utilized towards gaining financial freedom through passive income, indeed works like the hidden yet powerful engine propelling the flight of your financial dreams. This belief, profoundly grounded in your capabilities, fortifies your cradle of ambition and vision. Unequivocally, without poking into previous details, let's venture into this transformative process.

The journey begins by embracing an indomitable belief in our potential. This belief in ourselves becomes our guiding light, illuminating financial pathways that seemed obscure initially. It alleviates the stress induced by financial uncertainties. The consistent whispers of self-doubt are silenced as we amplify the voice of self-affirmation. A positive I can and I will attitude steers us towards financial independence.

Moving onto passive income, it is not an avenue for immediate riches, but a strategy that grows over time to create wealth. An integral factor for generating passive income is wisely leveraging one's existing resources, whether it be monetary assets, property, or unique skills. Detailed comprehension of these resources aids in uncovering their maximal utility. Also, the relentless belief in our ability to skillfully manage these resources is essential.

While passive income can be extracted from several means like real estate, investments, creative digital contents, or affiliate marketing, it demands strategic planning and effective execution. Here, believing in yourself to make informed and timely decisions refines the process.

As faith in our abilities strengthens, financial freedom stems up not just as a distant dream, but an achievable reality. This freedom is not confined to accumulating wealth or increasing net worth, but liberating oneself from the gloom of financial stress and deep-rooted economic fears. It thus leads to a life of abundance and prosperity, where your time is not tethered to making ends meet. In essence, it is living a life dictated not by financial obligations, but by personal desires and growth.

To wrap up, self-belief is the ideology; passive income is the method, and financial freedom is the coveted outcome. Necessitating quiet confidence and strategic planning, the journey towards financial independence through passive income is a testament to our belief in ourselves and our financial strategies. While the journey may be embellished with challenges, persistent belief and consistent efforts turn the pursuit of financial independence from a daunting quest into a fulfilling experience.

Believing in yourself and the power of self-confidence is not an airy-fairy, aspirational concept but indeed a driving force to experience real-world practical results. It's inherently about having faith in your abilities to learn new things, overcome challenges, take calculated risks, and achieve your goals. Self-belief is the cornerstone, serving as both the foundation and the fuel, for your journey to success. This mindset strengthens your decision-making process, improves problem-solving skills, and fosters resilience. Whether you're negotiating a business deal, starting a passion project, or aiming to generate passive income for financial freedom, believing in yourself plays a pivotal role in shaping your life's course.

Now, let's illustrate the concept of believing in oneself through a practical, real-world example. Meet Sam, a dynamic individual, who's always had an entrepreneurial spirit and a desire to attain financial freedom by generating passive income. However, this kind of venture was entirely new to him and surrounded by uncertainties. It didn't take long for him to realize the key to success lay within himself.

Sam always had a passion for fitness and noticed the growing trend of online fitness classes, catalyzed by the COVID-19 pandemic. He knew that creating a fitness-related app could be a potential source of passive income. But, designing an app was not in his comfort zone. Doubts started to surface; it was something he'd never done before - would he be able to do it?

Instead of succumbing to self-doubt, Sam chose to believe in his potential. He began learning about app development, sought advice from industry experts, and dug deep into market research. He confronted his apprehensions and transformed them into learning opportunities. After months of sheer hard work and determination, he turned his idea into a reality and launched a successful and groundbreaking fitness application.

The journey wasn't easy, but his self-belief and persistence paid off. His app started attracting users, and subscriptions began rolling in, generating a steady stream of passive income. This financial freedom enabled Sam to invest in other ventures, ensuring complete control over his financial destiny.

In conclusion, Sam's story shows how powerful believing in ourselves is. Sam was in a territory unknown to him, yet he succeeded in creating a passive income stream, achieving financial freedom. Like Sam, we all can direct our beliefs in our capabilities to translate our goals into realities, genuinely reinforcing that self-belief isn't just a conceptual ideology but a real-world practical asset.

CHAPTER 9: STRATEGIC PATH TOWARDS FINANCIAL SERENITY THROUGH MINDFUL PASSIVE INCOME

Mindfulness, an ancient practice promoting focused awareness and acknowledgment of feelings, thoughts, and sensations in the present moment, can be a potent tool for creating and managing passive income. This journey towards financial freedom demands a detailed understanding of financial matters which significantly blooms under mindful awareness.

Within the realm of finance, mindfulness enhances your ability to concentrate on your financial goals, systematically identifying each step required in the process. When investing in passive income streams like real estate, stocks, online businesses, or peer-to-peer lending, mindfulness supports precision and clarity for decision making. These investments potentially carry risk factors, therefore, practicing mindfulness enables one to maintain equanimity amidst volatile situations, stripping biases and triggering informed decisions.

Mindful budgeting is an essential aspect of preparing for passive income too. By practicing mindfulness while outlining expenditures and savings, it is possible to avoid unnecessary expenses and precisely allocate resources for potential investments.

Mindfulness facilitates learning and assimilation of new knowledge. The world of finance is vast and continuously evolving, necessitating continuous learning and adaptation. An important part of managing passive income is understanding how financial markets work, analyzing trends, and understanding investment principles. Mindfulness boosts such learning abilities, thereby optimizing decision-making capabilities for passive income management.

Finally, mindfulness encourages appreciation of the present moment. In the context of passive income, this means deriving a sense of accomplishment from each small financial win – each investment made, each revenue generated, which consequently fuels motivation. Generating income passively does not typically bear quick results. It is a progressive journey demanding patience and resilience. Thus, celebrating these small wins along the way is the art of mindfulness, progressively inching you closer to your financial freedom.

In conclusion, mindfulness promotes pragmatic decision making, effective learning, and appreciation of the journey in establishing passive income aiming at financial freedom. It isn't a magical solution but a strategic path towards attaining financial serenity incrementally yet assuredly.

Mindfulness is the psychological process of purposely bringing one's attention to experiences occurring in the present moment without judgment. It's the state of being completely aware, conscious of one's thought process, surroundings, and actions. Essentially, it refers to the utilization of full attention to our thoughts and feelings in the present moment, being fully aware of our current experiences, and not dwelling in the past or future. Mindfulness has its roots in ancient traditions, but it's also a crucial tool for navigating the complexities and pressures of modern life.

Practicing mindfulness helps us become aware of our thoughts and reactions and allows us to choose responses that align with our values and goals. It's primarily used to reduce stress, improve focus, enhance resilience, and navigate complicated emotions. In practical terms, mindfulness involves daily practices such as formal meditation, informal activities where one maintains awareness of their activities, and it can also involve structured mindfulness-based interventions.

In the realm of finance, especially concerning the concept of passive income, mindfulness is highly significant. Many individuals are seeking financial freedom, with passive income often seen as a key to this independence.

Let's dive into a story to exemplify this.

Meet Emily, a young professional working as an IT consultant. Despite earning a decent salary, Emily was always stressed about her financial future. She chanced upon an article about generating passive income as a way to achieve financial freedom and was intrigued. However, she knew that she would need a mindful approach to successfully navigate this new venture.

Emily started practicing mindfulness, training herself to live in the present and consciously experience her life. She took make mindful decisions about her finance. She became more aware of her spending habits, identifying areas where she was overspending, and noticing opportunities for saving and potential investments. Emily was fully present in her financial life.

Guided by her newfound mindfulness practice, Emily began exploring various sources of passive income. Rather than making hurried decisions fueled by anxiety about the future, she would deliberately consider each potential investment in the present moment. She focused not only on the potential return but also on her current financial status and future financial goals. Her decisions were not dictated by her desires, but by her present financial realities and well-analyzed future projections.

Eventually, Emily chose to invest in a rental property, a venture she had time to manage alongside her job and one that provided a stable source of passive income. With each mindful decision she made, she moved closer to financial freedom. Emily's journey towards financial independence is ongoing, but she credits her mindfulness practices for her progress.

In conclusion, mindfulness, although typically associated with stress management and improved focus, also has profound implications in our financial lives. It enables us to make well-informed decisions and to be fully engaged in our journey towards financial freedom, particularly in generating and managing passive income.

CHAPTER 10: HARNESSING THE ESSENCE OF PASSIVE INCOME FOR STEPPING TOWARDS FINANCIAL FREEDOM

Visualization of the strategic elements and implications encompassing the concept of passive income for financial freedom commences with the comprehension of this income type, which is a form of earning that requires minimal active involvement. It encompasses earnings from real estate investments, royalties, dividends, and more.

A more in-depth understanding of these streams creates an avenue for a thoughtfully structured financial plan. This includes a thorough assessment of the initial monetary requirement or the investment needed to trigger a steady flow of passive income, the predictable income growth rate, and the potential risks attached. Rather than considering these factors as standalone entities, visualizing them collectively helps to attain a holistic financial perspective.

Financial freedom manifests itself as the ultimate goal in this visualization journey. It is a stage wherein the earned passive income can comfortably cover the living expenses, leading to a life devoid of financial stress and constraints. Consequently, the visualization model should incorporate this dynamic of passive income concerning your monthly expenses. It forms a clear connection between the money flowing in passively and the sustained capability to meet financial obligations.

An additional protective layer in this financial model visualizes the emergency fund, a significant component in the journey towards financial freedom. Its importance lies in providing a safety net, financially catering to unexpected life events without hampering the stability of passive income.

Furthermore, the process of reinvestment is an integral chain in this visualization model. Reinvesting a part of the passive income has the potential to create more passive income streams, enhancing financial stability. Hence, the capital progression should represent a compounded growth model, amplifying the upright direction towards financial independence.

This visualization strategy is not static, but rather a fluid model that parallels the ebbs and flows of the financial market and the personal financial landscape. Therefore, amendments and adjustments are part of this visual journey, highlighting the need for ongoing financial education to add more depth to the understanding process. The continuously evolving financial plan morphs through stages, inherently matching the pace of life progression and financial goals.

By integrating all these elements into a comprehensive visualization model, financial freedom through passive income emerges as an attainable goal rather than an elusive dream. This model goes beyond the limited confines of numbers by incorporating the human factor, financial discipline, and adaptability towards market changes, paving way for a financially independent future.

Visualization is a powerful tool widely used in varying forms, ranging from data analysis to goal achievement, and even addressing personal milestones like financial freedom. In essence, visualization is the mental exercise of simulating a situation or outcome in your mind. It is fundamentally a form of mental rehearsal or daydreaming but backed by a specific intent or direction. Visualization is linked to improved motivation, confidence, and focus, all of which are necessary in achieving financial freedom.

Let's imagine the story of Jane. Jane is a hard-working woman in her mid-thirties. Despite having a well-paying job and living comfortably, she still feels a constant financial unease. The thought of depending solely on her 9 to 5 job until her old age seemed daunting. Jane decided to change her course, aiming for a financially stable future, even without her job income - Passive Income for Financial Freedom.

Jane starts by defining what financial freedom looks like to her. She desires to have a hefty savings account, own a few properties for a steady rental income, and some sound investments yielding a good return. With these goals visualized, she begins to observe daily those who have already reached such a milestone, learning from their habits and strategies.

Jane then starts visualizing herself as one of these successful people. She sees herself in a real estate agency, closing the deal on a rental property. She imagines the feeling of receiving rental income every month, just part of her overall passive income that keeps rolling in even when she's not actively working. Jane also starts visualizing herself reviewing and making smart investment decisions, watching those investments grow over time.

With these powerful and consistent visualizations, Jane becomes more and more motivated to transform her financial situation. She starts working smarter, saving more, taking the time to study investment and real estate markets. Over time, Jane's visualizations start to manifest in her reality. She sees her savings increasing, she buys her first real estate, and her investments begin to yield promising returns.

Eventually, Jane becomes financially free. She no longer depends only on her job for sustenance. She now has a consistent stream of income that even allows her to pursue her hobbies and interests without worrying about making ends meet. All because she had a vision and clearly visualized the financial freedom she wanted.

Jane's story is a classic example of how visualization can yield tangible outcomes. It Applies to virtually any real-world practical situation, including achieving your financial goals. Visualization provides the motivation, confidence, and focus necessary to transform your financial reality and achieve financial freedom.

Chapter 11: Crafting Your Action Plan: The Blueprint to Passive Income for Financial Freedom

In this riveting chapter, we will propel you into the realm of action. But, before we delve into that, allow us to illustrate what we mean by an Action Plan.

An action plan is your personal compass, your roadmap, guiding you towards your destination - in this case, passive income for financial freedom. This plan will make the difference between aimless wandering and traveling with purpose. It's a structured strategy that specifies the exact steps you'll need to take, providing a clear understanding of your target, and how precisely to get there.

If you're feeling the pressure, remember this - the beauty of an action plan is in its flexibility. You have the ability to modify and personalize it as you gain more experience, or as circumstances change. This isn't a rigid rulebook, it's a strategic guide that will evolve with you.

Why is this pertinent? Because financial freedom isn't just about making money. It's about proactive, conscious decision-making - deciding where to invest your time and resources, how to mitigate risks, and how to create sustainable, long-term passive income streams.

Now, let's get excited. Because we now stand at the cusp of translating thoughts into tactile operations - moving from contemplation to action. We are about to introduce you to your action plan.

Imagine yourself embarking on a ground-breaking voyage, a journey towards structuring your passive income and establishing financial freedom. This isn't a haphazard journey, though, but a meticulously planned, step-by-step trek specifically designed to lead you to success. With every forward step, the fog of uncertainty will begin to lift, and with every maneuver made in accordance with the action plan, you will find yourself firmly placed on the path of financial freedom.

In this chapter, we will be your torchbearers in the world of passive income generation. We will lay out the stepping stones for creating a plan so clear and detailed, you will feel equipped and inspired to step into action.

Our aim is to transform you from a passive reader to an active implementer of strategies that will lead you straight to financial freedom. So brace yourself for an exhilarating journey, as we begin to chart your course towards the revolutionary world of passive income and financial freedom!

Are you ready to turn the page and begin shaping your financial future? If so, let's dive into the world of action planning - your first port of call on this voyage towards passive income and financial independence. Your guide toward forging a dynamic, prosperous future awaits within these pages. Let's get started, explorer!

In the previous chapters, we identified three major elements that are of great importance in successfully achieving financial freedom through passive income. Let's revisit, recollect, and embrace these solutions once again.

1. The Mind-blowing Solution: The first solution that we inspected was the diversification of investments to amplify potential returns. Turning an eye to real estate, e-commerce, smartphone apps, and cryptocurrencies, this strategy calls upon the adoption of innovative financial strategies. This solution recognizes the power of low-effort, high-yield investments and the importance of embracing new technologies and markets for sound investment and significant income generation.

2. Career Solution: The second solution underscores the importance of mastering the art of passive income generation as a career. This solution acknowledges the necessity to plan, persist, and optimize resources, gradually shifting from traditional methods to innovative

systems of income generation that require minimal consistency of input.

3. Spiritual Solution: The third and last solution delves into aligning financial pursuits with individual spirituality. It draws strength from teachings of mindfulness and shared prosperity, advocating for patience, persistence, and a keen realization of the impermanence of everything, including financial status.

These three solutions, combined holistically, can pave the way for a promising and prosperous journey towards financial freedom through passive income.

The triad of these solutions doesn't merely target your financial growth but also amalgamates your career aspirations and spiritual mindset to invigorate a unique, viable, and rewarding path leading towards financial independence. This path, if traversed with dedication and smart work, ultimately leads to peace of mind and sustainable financial stability.

As we proceed further in the book, a comprehensive integration of these solutions will be provided to generate one effective plan of action unlike any other, setting the stage for your saunter towards financial security - your journey towards the realization of your dreams.

Exciting times and enticing lessons are just around the corner. Keep reading, keep learning and keep inching towards your financial freedom the passive way.

CHAPTER 11: THE HARMONIZED PROSPERITY APPROACH: A COMPREHENSIVE SOLUTION FOR PASSIVE INCOME GENERATION

To synthesize these three solutions and mold them into one coherent, actionable strategy, we must first discern the connectedness and complementarity between them.

1. First, cultivate the Mind-blowing Solution by broadening your investment outlook. Dive into unchartered waters of real estate, e-commerce, smartphone apps, and cryptocurrencies without hesitance but with due diligence. This begins your journey towards generating various modes of passive income, creating a safety net and a buffer for progressive financial growth.

2. Simultaneously, remodel your career path aligning with the Career Solution. Start by making a gradual shift from conventional income methods towards passive ones, emphasizing planning, persistence, and optimizing resources. Craft your career so it becomes a vehicle towards financial independence, not just a means to earn a monthly paycheck.

3. Lastly, incorporating the Spiritual Solution is crucial to sustain the results from the first two steps and to attain true financial freedom. Adopt a mindset of patience, persistence, and utmost focus on the goal of financial security. Harness the power of mindfulness and shared prosperity to create a wholesome and fulfilling path towards your financial goals.

As the name suggests, the Harmonized Prosperity Approach entails harmonizing your financial pursuits with your career aspirations and personal well-being. It's about bringing together a diversified finance approach, career reimagining, and spiritual tweaking to achieve a life that balances wealth generation with career satisfaction and spiritual serenity.

Step into the realm of financial stability and peace where work isn't merely a chore but rather a manifestation of your dreams and aspirations. For this, the blend of the triad method is not just essential but indeed the only way forward.

In Integrated Pathways to Wealth, I propose a comprehensive methodology which effectively addresses the quest for passive income and consequently, financial freedom. This solution combines three distinct strategies — Diversified Investing, Career Revolution, and Inner Wealth Unlocking. Each strategy plays a crucial role and their synergistic interaction multiplies their individual impacts to formulate a holistic solution.

Diversified Investing engenders a broad array of income sources. This strategy cultivates resilience in the face of economic uncertainties and helps maintain a steady cash flow. However, it requires a deep understanding of various market dynamics and prudent risk management.

Career Revolution implicates a career restructuring focusing on passive income generation. It involves leveraging skills, knowledge, and personal strengths to create financial streams that require minimal active involvement.

Lastly, Inner Wealth Unlocking anchors the whole approach with a stable mental and emotional state. A harmonious internal world motivates progressive financial choices, guides wise decision-making, and grounds us against unfavorable market conditions.

In synergy, these three strategies lead to an efficient revenue-generating mechanism: diversified investments create multiple income streams, the revolutionary career approach ensures these streams align with your skills and passions, and the unlocking of inner wealth guarantees financial decisions' alignment with personal fulfillment.

Integrated Pathways to Wealth provides a sustainable and prosperous path to financial freedom and personal satisfaction. By synergizing various strategies, it offers a holistic approach that allows anyone to reimagine their financial journey, create multiple income streams, and ultimately attain financial freedom.

CHAPTER 12: 30-DAY SMART GOALS WITH KPIS AND MILESTONES FOR INTEGRATED PATHWAYS TO WEALTH

Week 1: Diversified Investing
SMART Goal: By the end of the first week, identify, research, and select at least three diverse potential passive income sources to invest in.

Key Performance Indicators (KPIs):
- Number of potential income sources identified and evaluated.
- Amount of resources allocated to each source.

Milestones:
- Day 1-3: Identify various potential income sources.
- Day 4-5: Conduct in-depth research on each selected source.
- Day 6-7: Finalize, decide on the optimal three sources to invest in.

Week 2: Investment Strategy & Portfolio Creation
SMART Goal: By end of 2nd week, create a detailed investment strategy for chosen income sources and set up your investment portfolio.

KPIs:

- Completion of a detailed investment strategy.
- Successful setup of the investment portfolio.

Milestones:
- Day 8-10: Devise a comprehensive investment strategy for the chosen income sources.
- Day 11-14: Implement your investment strategy and set up your diversified investment portfolio.

Week 3: Career Revolution

SMART Goal: End of Week 3, identify specific skills/knowledge that can be leveraged for passive income generation and outline a strategy to implement.

KPIs:
- Number of potential career skill sets identified.
- Creation of a comprehensive action plan.

Milestones:
- Day 15-17: Identification of skills and areas of expertise ideally suited for passive income creation.
- Day 18-21: Formulation of a transformation strategy from conventional job role to leveraging personal strengths for passive income.

Week 4: Inner Wealth Unlocking

SMART Goal: Develop mindfulness strategies and exercises by the end of the 4th week to maintain mental and emotional stability while implementing and managing the new passive income strategies.

KPIs:
- Number of mindfulness strategies developed.
- Regularity in practicing mindfulness exercises.

Milestones:
- Day 22 and 23: Learn the basics of mindfulness and its application for financial well-being.
- Day 24-26: Develop specific mindfulness strategies applicable to personal financial scenario.

- Day 27-30: Regularly practice the devised mindfulness exercises and incorporate them into daily life.

By the end of these 30 days, you should have a diversified passive income portfolio aligned with your skills and a mindfulness strategy to maintain harmony while managing your financial affairs.

Title: 30 Day Action Plan for Success

Day 1: Start with market research. Investigate various passive income sources that align with your interests and skills.

Day 2: Deepen your research on your selected sources. Review their success rates, intake methods, and average income generation.

Day 3: Finalize your selection of three diverse passive income sources based on their usability and potential profitability.

Day 4: Allocate resources to each selected income source. Create a cost-analysis for each investment.

Day 5: Develop an investment strategy for the first source. This includes setting goals, risk assessment, and deciding a timeline.

Day 6: Develop an investment strategy for the second source.

Day 7: Develop an investment strategy for the third source.

Day 8: Implement your plan for the first source. This could involve buying stocks, setting up a blog, etc, depending on the nature of the source.

Day 9: Monitor the progress of the first source. Arrange your findings in a spreadsheet or portfolio manager.

Day 10: Implement your plan for the second source.

Day 11: Monitor the progress of the second source and maintain records similarly.

Day 12: Implement your plan for the third source.

Day 13: Monitor the progress of the third source, maintain records.

Day 14: Review the performance of all three sources. Make any necessary adjustments to enhance performance.

Day 15: Analyze your current professional skillset. List out skills that can be monetized as a source of passive income. Brainstorm ways to leverage these skills. This could involve providing consulting services, creating an e-course, or writing an e-book, etc.

Day 16: Make a detailed analysis of your professional skills. This includes identifying the skills you have honed over the years that are relevant for generating passive income.

Day 17: Identify various platforms where you can leverage these skills. This could be eBook platforms, freelancing websites, or creating an online course.

Day 18: Decide on the platform that aligns with your skills. For instance, if you've chosen to write an eBook, select the genre and the platform where you would sell it.

Day 19: Start creating content for your platform. If it's an eBook, start your draft. If it's a course, start creating a module list.

Day 20: Continue creating content. Schedule your time and set a target for daily content creation.

Day 21: Create a marketing plan for your content. This includes identifying the target audience, promotional channels, and promotional strategies.

Day 22: Create a SMART (Specific, Measurable, Achievable, Relevant and Time-Bound) goal for this passive income venture. Develop KPIs (Key Performance Indicators) to track your progress.

Day 23: Implement your promotional strategies. This can start with a social media announcement or an email campaign.

Day 24: Engage with your audience. Reply to their comments, feedback, or queries. Keep the buzz alive.

Day 25: Fine-tune your content based on the audience response. The audience's feedback gives you valuable inputs on what they need.

Day 26: Finalize your content. Make it audience-friendly and value-packed.

Day 27: Launch your product in a manner that creates maximum buzz. Use all your promotional channels effectively.

Day 28: Evaluate the response with respect to your KPIs. Make note of achievements and areas that need improvement.

Day 29: Continue your engagement activities. Personal interaction makes the audience feel valued and increases credibility.

Day 30: Review all three passive income ventures and compare their success. Make necessary tweaks in your future plan based on this comparison. Identify the most successfully implemented venture and further expand it.

Detailed Daily Actions
Day 1 - Starting With Market Research

Step 1: Start your day by defining the goal of your market research. It helps to align your purpose and set the direction for your research. This goal could be finding passive income sources that are in line with your interests, skills, and financial projections.

Step 2: Dedicate some time to understand the methodology of market research. Instead of diving in blindly, knowing the hows and whys can greatly simplify the process. Use online resources to understand what passive income is, its different types, and how each works. It is crucial for the informed selection of the income source later in the plan.

Step 3: Now, start looking for passive income sources. A good starting point could be online business blogs, financial advice websites, or forums discussing passive income. Make a list as you go along, noting down their basic characteristics.

Step 4: Deep dive into the top three to five sources you found interesting. Here, you would want to consider aspects like, 'What skills are required?', 'What is the initial cost and expected return on investment?', 'How much time and effort is needed on a daily basis?' and 'What is the overall profitability?' This step is essential for a fact-based decision, allowing you to eliminate options that don't fit your personal circumstances or ambitions.

Step 5: Repeat the research process for each potential income source. The more you know about each choice, the better. You aim not to leave any room for surprises down the line.

Step 6: End your day with a reflection on the day's work. Remember that you are taking the steps towards financial freedom. Let this push you forward, motivate you to continue the journey.

By the end of Day 1, you have started the path on your financial freedom journey. It is always going to be the most challenging, as you excavate unfamiliar terrains. But remember, every step you take brings you closer to your goal of financial independence.

Let's move onto Day 2 with the same enthusiasm - the journey has only just begun! Keep the momentum going - you're off to a promising start. Remember, the path to success is paved with continued effort and a clear vision. You are on your way to creating a life of financial freedom, and each day is a brick in the foundation of your success.

Day 2 - Unearthing Profitable Opportunities

Step 1: Start your day with refreshing brain teasers. Make sure you are in the right frame of mind to delve deeper into your selected potential passive income sources.

Why: Beginning your day with activities that activate your brain cells can stimulate your mental faculties and prepare your mind for analytical tasks, which will be crucial for today's research.

Step 2: Allocate a quiet workspace and define your research parameters. Define your 'opportunity criteria' - these are specific characteristics you're looking for in passive income sources. The criteria may include scalability, initial investment required, necessary skills, and time commitment.

Why: A classified workspace and clearly defined parameters will streamline your research, making it more focused and efficient. Choosing your criteria ensure that the ensuing shortlist of opportunities matches your resources, skills, and personal preferences.

Step 3: Proceed with an in-depth examination of each income source on your list. Investigate various factors such as entry barriers, profitability, sustainability, risks, and market conditions. Online sources such as online entrepreneurial forums, financial podcasts, and expert articles can be useful.

Why: Understanding each element in detail narrows down your choices as it will enable you to identify which passive income sources are viable, profitable, and align with your interests and skills for achieving financial freedom.

Step 4: Compare your findings with your opportunity criteria defined earlier. Eliminate any sources that do not align with your criteria.

Why: Prioritizing an opportunity that meets your goals and resources enhances the chances of turning a passive income idea into a steady stream of income.

Step 5: Review the remaining opportunities and create a top three list based on profitability and alignment with your skills.

Why: Sorting your list helps you to focus on your most promising prospects first, ensuring maximum return for your time investment.

As you complete Day 2, remember that the journey to passive income and financial freedom is just as much about the voyage as it is about reaching the destination. Cherish the learning curve and resilience you're building. Success is born out of dedication and consistency - don't be discouraged if today felt overwhelming, you're laying the groundwork for a future of financial independence! Each task is a brick in your financial fortress. Carry on, because you're building something remarkable, brick by brick!

Day 3: Selection of Passive Income Sources

Day 3 of your 30-Day Action Plan for Financial Freedom is all about honing in on the strengths of your diverse passive income sources and finalizing your selection. This is a significant step towards success as it guides where your resources will be directed for the most potent return on investment.

Step 1: Review Your Potential Sources
Begin by reviewing your potential income sources list from the previous day. Think about the specifics of each: their associated risks, your ability to control them, the possible return on investment, and how they align with your long-term financial goals.

Step 2: Consider Time-Investment Balance
Consider the required time-to-investment balance for each source. Passive income should ideally require little to no work after the initial setup phase. So, balance these requirements against potential returns.

Step 3: Match Sources to Personal Interests
Critically analyze how well these sources align with your passion and interests. If you love what you do, it significantly reduces the chance of burnout and increases the potential for long-term success.

Step 4: Diversification Check
Ensure that there is enough diversification among your chosen sources. This will spread your risk across different assets and markets. Your chosen sources should work in harmony but not be overly reliant on each other.

Step 5: Final Selection
After considering all factors, select your final three passive income sources. This is your first active step towards wealth creation. Commit your decision to paper and mentally prepare yourself for the exciting journey that lies ahead.

Each of these steps edges you closer towards financial freedom. By consciously selecting passive income sources aligned with your interests and long-term financial goals, and ensuring adequate diversification, you'll set up a strong foundation for your wealth-building journey.

Remember, success comes to those who plan meticulously and act decisively. Continue dedicating yourself to this process and staying open to learning, and you will begin to see your financial landscape transform.

As you lay your head down tonight, remind yourself that you're three days into a life-changing plan. Every step, no matter how minor it may seem, contributes to a larger picture of financial freedom and success. Stay committed, dedicated, and always keep your aims in sight. Let's march towards Day 4, buoyed with the excitement and promise of the prosperity that lies ahead!

Day 4: Allocating and Distributing Resources

On day 4 of our 30-day action plan, we will be allocating and distributing our resources across the three diverse passive income sources that we've selected. This step is a critical part of the journey towards financial freedom, as it ensures that your money is utilized efficiently.

Step 1: Estimate Your Total Investable Capital
Identify the total amount of money you're prepared to invest in your passive income venture. This could be savings, funds you're prepared to borrow, or income from other sources. Understanding your total investable capital will help you allocate money effectively among your three chosen sources.

Step 2: Evaluate the Risk and Profit Potential
For each chosen income source, consider its risk level and potential return based on your research from Days 2 and 3. A well-balanced portfolio consists of income sources of varying risk to ensure your financial safety.

Step 3: Allocate Resources

Based on your risk evaluation, allocate a percentage of your total investable capital to each of your three income sources. A commonly used rule of thumb is to subtract your age from 100 to find out what percentage of your portfolio should be invested in riskier (typically higher return) assets.

Step 4: Finalize Your Investment Plan
Outline your final investment plan. State how much capital you plan to invest in each source, and a timeline for when you expect returns. This becomes your strategic guideline for the remaining days.

Why is this day important for your financial success?
Allocating your resources thoughtfully is a crucial step in creating diversified passive income. A well-diversified portfolio can help you earning returns even if one or two investments do not perform as expected. Balancing risk is key to long-term financial stability and growth, which is why devoting time and reasoning in this stage can significantly boost your chances of achieving financial freedom.

End Message:
Remember, in this journey towards financial freedom, every step is a progression. Today you've laid the groundwork for your diversified portfolio by allocating your resources logically and tactfully. Keep going! With each meticulous preparation, you are one step closer to your financial freedom. Every single day matters, and so does your focused effort. You're doing fantastic, and your future self will thank you for the wise decisions you're making today. Keep moving forward - your dream of financial freedom is within your grasp!

Day 5: Allocating Resources for Optimal Returns

Day 5 of our 30-day action plan is dedicated to resource allocation. At this stage, you have already researched and selected three potential passive income sources that align with your skills and interests. Now, it's time to decide how your available resources should be divided among these sources.

1: Identify Your Resources

Start by taking stock of what resources you have at your disposal. This could be financial resources, time, and/or your skills. Understanding what you have is crucial for deciding how much you can afford to invest in your passive income sources.

Step 2: Understand Your Risk Tolerance

Next, determine your risk tolerance. This will dictate how you allocate resources, as certain passive income sources could be riskier than others. For example, investing in stocks can potentially yield high returns, but the risk is also high. Alternatively, investing in something like real estate or a high-yield savings account might have lower returns, but also lower risk.

Step 3: Allocate Resources

Now that you understand your resources and risk tolerance, divide your resources among your three passive income sources. If you're risk-averse, you might want to allocate more resources to safer bets. If you're comfortable with risks for higher returns, you might invest more in high-risk, high-return options.

Step 4: Document Your Decisions

Keep track of how you've allocated your resources. This helpful for future reference and to make adjustments down the line.

Today's actions are critical for your path to financial freedom. By carefully allocating resources, you can construct a diversified portfolio of passive income sources. This diversification reduces risk and increases the potential for overall success, as you're not relying on a single income source. Instead, you're spreading your investment over a range of opportunities, which improves the odds of finding a successful venture.

Remember, the journey to financial freedom is a marathon, not a sprint. Stay motivated, keep learning, and remain consistent with your efforts. You are building the foundation of your financial future one brick at a time. Don't rush, take your time to build strong and sturdy, so it can stand the test of time and provide you a steady stream of income for the years to come. Celebrate this process because you are taking steps that many are afraid to take. Keep going! Tomorrow holds another opportunity for growth and success.

Day 6

On Day 6 of our 30-Day SMART Goals with KPIs and Milestones for Integrated Pathways to Wealth plan, we focus on developing a comprehensive investment strategy for the first passive income source. This day helps with wealth creation as part of your journey toward financial freedom.

Step 1: Goal Setting
Start by establishing your financial goals for that source. Defining your goals is critical as it provides you with a clear purpose and destination. Remember, your goals should be SMART (Specific, Measurable, Achievable, Relevant, and Time-bound). Today, you will establish your long-term (1 year), medium-term (6 months), and short-term (1 month) goals for this passive income source.

Step 2: Understanding the Source
Become intimately acquainted with your chosen source. If you are investing in stocks, this will be the time to understand the company's performance. If it's a real estate investment, understand the market conditions and future trends. For a blog or online platform, understand your audience and their needs.

Step 3: Risk Assessment
On Day 6, you also assess the potential risks associated with your chosen passive income source. Every investment comes with a degree of risk. Your job today is to identify those threats and devise ways to mitigate them. This could be anything from market volatility, technological disruptions, or shifts in consumer behavior.

Step 4: Outline Your Investment Roadmap
This will be your step-by-step plan detailing how, when, and where you will allocate resources for this source. It will comprise the amount of money you want to invest initially, desired rate of return,

period for which you want to stay invested, and your exit strategy. Use your medium-term and short-term goals to guide this outline.

Step 5: Evaluate and Refine
After outlining your investment strategy, take the time to evaluate it. Review it against your threat analysis and overall financial plan. You might find areas that need tweaking. Make adjustments where necessary; flexibility is the key to a successful investment strategy.

Today's tasks build your foundation for successfully implementing the chosen passive income source, guiding you closer to financial freedom. Remember, investment is a journey, not a sprint.

Success is a journey that is different for everyone. Today, you've made significant progress. Keep up the excellent work because, at the end of this road, financial freedom awaits. It might seem a little overwhelming right now, but trust in the process and your ability to succeed!

Day 7 - Final Decision Day & Investment Allocation

Objective of the Day: To make a final decision on the three diverse income sources that will set you on the path to financial freedom and to designate a calculated amount of resources to each.

Step 1: Comparing Potential Income Sources
Begin your day with a thorough review of all the potential income sources you have researched over the past six days. Detail the pros and cons of each and rank them according to their viability for your situation. This step is crucial because you are streamlining your options and homing in on the ones which are most likely to hand you ownership of your financial future.

Step 2: Selecting the Top Three
From your ranked list, select the top three income sources. This diversification is key to mitigating risk; if one source underperforms, you can still count on the other two. Consider the full range - investing, real estate, online business, stock market, digital assets, or intellectual property royalties. A well-diversified portfolio is more

resistant to market fluctuations and is often a major stepping stone towards financial freedom.

Step 3: Allocating Resources
Having selected your income sources, it's now time to allocate resources which could be capital, time, and effort. Depending on the nature of the sources selected, the allocation will vary. If it's an online business, for example, more time might be needed for creation and set-up. If it's real estate or stock market, capital allocation will be the major focus. This step is crucial, as a calculated investment will be the bloodline of your income sources, helping each to thrive and generate returns.

Step 4: Initial Action Plan
Create a preliminary action plan for each source, laying out the road map for what needs to be done from this point forward, including time frames and goals. This setup allows you to plan ahead and align your tasks with the desired goal of achieving passive income.

Step 5: Reflect
End the day reflecting on the progress made so far. Recognize that you're laying the groundwork for making this financial dream of passive income a reality.

Day 7 is critical in your journey toward financial freedom. It takes your research and thought from the previous six days and materializes it into a practical, feasible decision. By this stage, you've equipped yourself with a vision and resources for three financial sources that, with diligence and perseverance, will strive to generate perpetual income streams. This day solidifies that initial step on your road to financial self-sufficiency, setting the stage for action from Day 8 onwards.

You've made it through the first week! This journey to financial freedom is as much about resilience and determination as it is about smart decisions. Keep the focus, hold on to your perseverance, and remember – Rome wasn't built in a day. This is just the beginning; let's ride the wave of financial liberation together!

Day 8: Activation of Your First Passive Income Source

On Day 8, the initial aim is to activate your first chosen passive income source. The primary steps include execution of the investment strategy, operationalization of resources, and launching the investment activity.

Step 1: Initiating the Investment Process
The first and foremost step is to initiate the process involved in your selected passive income source. For instance, if you have chosen rental properties, it's time to buy your first property until the specified budget. If it's stock market investing, begin by buying your first batch of shares. This step is crucial as it marks your official entry into the world of passive income generation.

Step 2: Operationalization of Resources
Here, you will operate the resources identified and allocated on Day 4. This may involve deploying manpower, technological resources, or financial assets to kick-start your chosen investment process. An example is setting up your website and writing your first blog post if you've chosen blogging as your income source. It will help to streamline the deployment processes, contributing to efficient management and utilization of resources.

Step 3: Manage Risk
As you launch, ensure rudimentary risk management measures are in place. These should be elements of your investment strategy devised earlier. Methods can be diversifying investments, setting stop loss levels for stock trading, or insuring your rental property.

Step 4: Launch Your Investment
The final step is to launch your investment activity officially. This could mean publishing your blog posts, listing your property for rent, or buying your first shares in the stock market.

By activating your first source of passive income, you set the wheel in motion towards achieving financial freedom. This day allows you to utilize all your planning and lays the foundation for your wealth-building journey.

Remember, embarking on this journey requires courage and determination, and you have taken that first formidable step. Keep in mind that this is a long-term journey, and success may not be instant, but consistency and patience will lead you to the financial freedom you are seeking. Look at each step as a learning experience. Now, let's bring the same enthusiasm to Day 9. The journey to financial freedom has just begun, and remember, the only impossible journey is the one you never begin. Stay motivated!

Day 9 - Monitoring Progress and Assessment

Step 1: Login Into Your Investment Portfolio

The first step of the day is to log in into your investment platform, where you've implemented the plan for the first passive income source from Day 8. This could be a brokerage account for stocks you've bought, a blog you've created, etc. Regular monitoring is essential as it will not just indicate the current status but will also give you a grasp of the pace at which your investment is progressing.

Step 2: Track The Performance

Once you login, your primary task is to track the performance of your investment. Check the current value, any dividends or returns it generated. This step will provide you with objective data about how your investment is performing in real-time. It will highlight whether your investment is aligned with your initial expectations, providing practical insight into your passive income generation.

Step 3: Document The Progress

Documenting the insights from the previous step is crucial. Use a spreadsheet or a portfolio tracking tool to monitor all progress details accurately. Note the current value, any profit you made, any losses, or significant changes. Documentation is an invaluable tool as it helps you follow the growth trend of your investment and make data-driven decisions later.

Step 4: Analyze and Reflect

Analyze the documented data. Reflect on the return on investment, any financial fluctuations, market trends, and your initial expectations. This step serves as the foundation for future decision making. It helps you determine whether you need to adjust your strategies, stay consistent, or rethink your investment.

In terms of supporting your journey to financial freedom, this day is indispensable. Monitoring your progress transparently and objectively allows you to learn from your actions. It helps you understand the workings of your selected passive income source and enables you to eventually master it, bringing you closer to your goal of financial freedom.

Remember, success is a journey, not a destination. Every step you take brings you closer to your financial goals. Stay patient, stay persistent, and remember that the key to wealth accumulation is in understanding the process, not just enjoying the result. So, keep up the good work, and think about how far you've come already. There's light at the end of the tunnel, and you're relentlessly moving towards it!

Day 10 - Setting Your Second Income Source in Motion

Day 10 is pivotal in your path towards financial freedom; you will be initiating your second passive income source, setting the foundation for a diversified income portfolio.

Step 1: Brush Up on Your Research

Begin your day by revisiting the information you have gathered on your second income source. Remember that thorough knowledge and understanding are the keys to leverage any investment. Refresh your recall of the feasibility, profitability potential, common pitfalls, and, most importantly, the steps to implementation of this specific source.

Step 2: Laying the Foundation

Based on the strategy designed earlier, start implementing actions one at a time. For example, if your second passive income source is to create an e-course, your first steps could be deciding on a course topic based on your expertise, identifying the target audience, and setting up your course outline.

Step 3: Start Building

Once you have laid out the foundation, start building up. Continuing with the e-course example, this could mean developing the modules, sourcing or creating materials, and setting up the platform where you'll host the course.

Step 4: Troubleshoot

As you progress with your set up, you're likely to encounter challenges. Troubleshoot in real-time to avoid larger issues down the road. Don't hesitate to refer back to your research, seek expert advice, use community forums or take online tutorials to resolve issues.

Step 5: Review and Adjust

Before the day ends, take time to review what you have accomplished. Evaluate if you've been able to stick to your plan, how effectively you've executed today's tasks, and where you stand on your timeline. Consider any necessary adjustments you have to make in your forthcoming steps.

Setting up your second income source is the continuation of diversifying your income flow. Diversified income not only helps in risk management but also increases capacity for wealth creation. Today's effort is your ticket to generating consistent wealth and inching closer to financial freedom.

And remember, success is like a mosaic, built one small piece at a time. So, keep up the good work. You're building something incredible and making consistent progress towards your journey to financial independence. Each step, no matter how small, is a stride towards success. Your dedication and efforts today will reap rewards tomorrow. You're doing an incredible job, so keep forging ahead!

Day 11: Active Implementation and Monitoring of the Second Passive Income Source

On Day 11, your focus shifts from the planning phase to the implementation phase of the secondary passive income source.

1. Step 1: Review Your Investment Strategy: Begin your day by revisiting the comprehensive investment strategy you prepared on Day 6. This could include, for instance, investing in dividend stocks or setting up a dropshipping business. Review the associated risks, expected return, and investment timeline for the second income source.

2. Step 2: Begin Implementation: Based on the strategy you formulated, initiate the procedure. If you decided to invest in dividend stocks, start by purchasing a set of promising stocks from the market. If dropshipping was your preference, create your online store, choose products, and find suppliers.

3. Step 3: Record Your Actions: Document every action you take. This helps in forming a reference document and mitigates potential future challenges. Keep records of each transaction, conversation, and agreement.

4. Step 4: Set Up Monitoring Tools: Depending on the nature of your source, set up a system to track the progress of your investment. For stocks, a portfolio tracking application might be ideal. For a dropshipping business, use analytics tools to track visitors, conversions, and sales.

5. Step 5: Make Your First Assessment: At the end of the day, take a step back, look at your progress. This will help identify any changes that need to be made immediately, ensuring you control the direction your investment moves towards.

This day plays a critical role in your journey towards financial freedom. It sets the stage for a secondary income stream and the simultaneous progression of multiple sources ensures you're not only diversifying your sources but also maximizing the potential for passive income generation. Today's activities teach you to juggle multiple investments, an essential skill for successful investors.

Completing Day 11 not only brings you one step closer to your financial objectives but also instills confidence that can propel you to keep moving forward in your endeavor for financial freedom. The feeling of having not one but two potential income streams is invigorating and signifies the unfolding of new financial possibilities.

Remember, great things come from small beginnings. Faith and perseverance are your greatest allies on this journey. Keep going!

Day 12: Execution of Third Income Source

The twelfth day in our quest for financial freedom through passive income is dedicated to the implementation of our plan for the third chosen source. Here's a detailed plan of action:

Step 1: Finalize Strategy
Revisit the investment strategy curated specifically for this third income source. Reconfirm its feasibility, compatibility with personal interests and alignment with the overall passive income goal. This step is crucial for creating a safety net for your investments.

Step 2: Invest
Put your strategy into action. This could entail procuring an income-generating rental property, making an investment in a high-yield index fund, or buying an existing online business; it completely depends on what suits your overall plan. Remember, the investment should be in line with the financial limit set for this particular source.

Step 3: Setup Passive Operation
For this investment to truly act as a 'passive' income, you need to ensure its operation is as automated as possible. Enlist expert assistance if needed. For example, hire a property management company for the rental property or use robo-advisor for index fund management.

Step 4: Record

Maintain an accurate record of all the transactions, contracts, or any pertinent documents involved in this investment. This could assist in future discretions or problems.

Step 5: Share Details
If your third source involves a business, make sure to inform your existing clients, your network, and the customers about your new venture. Leverage social media and promotional activities to ensure a wide reach.

Step 6: Monitor & Reflect
While this day is primarily about kickstarting your third income source, it's also about reflection. Reflect on the journey you've undertaken so far; the learning, the improvements, the adaptations. Remember to not get so lost in producing that you forget about learning and improving.

By the end of Day 12, you'll be on a path toward increased income diversity, risk mitigation, and passive revenue stream. Implementing this third source helps in buffering your financial safety net and gets you closer to the dream of financial freedom.

Finally, remember, beginnings can be challenging and wrought with uncertainties, but it's these bold steps that pave the way for the extraordinary. The courage you're showing in taking control of your financial future, exploring new arenas, and persisting even when it's uncomfortable is commendable. Remember, each day is a new stepping stone to your financial freedom. Stay diligent, stay focused, and keep going!

Day 13 awaits you with new learning, don't stop! You are not just creating multiple income sources, but a whole new future. Keep going!

Day 13: Activation of Third Passive Income Source

Morning Routine:
1. Begin your morning with a brief review of your plan for activating the third source of passive income. This would be an overview of

your investment strategy. Remember that your choice of this source was a result of careful selection and thorough analysis, lending credibility and potential to this journey.

2. Devote a segment of your morning to mindfulness practice. This is to ensure your mental health and focus are prioritized, enabling clear thought-processes and decision-making abilities throughout the day.

Prime Actions:
1. Start implementing your investment strategy for your third passive source. The step-by-step execution could range from setting up an online course to purchasing real estate, depending on your chosen avenue. Remember to follow your pre-determined plan to avoid last-minute decisions or changes. This consistency allows you to track progress and possibly predict future outcomes.

2. As the process unfolds, keep a record of each step taken, all expenses incurred, and any minor or major changes from your initial plan. This real-time documentation forms the basis of your monitoring system, permitting a comprehensive overview and understanding of the functioning of this source.

3. Reach out to your professional network, mentors or peers within this field, notifying them about your new venture. Not only does this create a support network, but also potential collaborations or partnerships. This level of intricacy included in your frontier endeavor helps in maximizing outcomes and minimizing risks.

Quality Checks:
1. Take some time to review your day's work in the evening. Cross-check all your steps and actions against your strategic plan. Make sure the actions you've taken match your plans and the resources allocated. Your self-check mechanism acts as a preventive measure against any deviations or misappropriations, paving the path for smooth operation.

Reflection:

1. At the end of the day, reflect on the day's undertakings, focusing on learnings and any shortcomings. Your ability to recognize and rectify mistakes promptly would help convert potential pitfalls into stepping stones.

Tying it Together:
Implementing your plan for the third source activates a new income stream that adds to your growing portfolio. With each source that you activate, your financial freedom steps closer, as fresh passive income not only contributes to your total earning but also diversifies your portfolio, spreading risks and potentially increasing overall returns.

End of the Day Message:
You've made significant progress in these thirteen days, stepping out of your comfort zone, and daring to venture into unfamiliar paths for the sake of financial liberation. Remember, every action you take brings you closer to your goal. This journey may challenge you, but always remember the sweet taste of financial freedom that awaits at the end. Here's to the brave new investor in you! Keep going, the best is yet to come!

Day 14: Performance Evaluation and Adjustments

On Day 14 of our 30-Day Action Plan for Success, your primary task is to assess your passive income sources' performance and make necessary adjustments to maximize productivity.

Step 1: Evaluate - Start with a comprehensive review of the three passive income sources implemented thus far. This encompasses checking the responses and returns you're receiving, and compiling the data into one report. This can be essential in finding areas of improvement, identifying patterns and surprises, and keeping track of the progress that you are making on your journey to financial freedom.

Step 2: Interpret Data - Interpreting the data is an important next step. This includes a detailed breakdown of how much income you've generated, the strengths and weaknesses that you have observed in your strategies, and discerning any obvious successes or failures. This step will guide your decisions moving forward and help you focus on efficiency.

Step 3: Compare and Contrast - The next step is to compare and contrast each income source's performance. It's essential to note how each is contributing to your financial freedom journey, and whether one source needs more attention or adjustment than another. This step helps in understanding the dynamics of your passive income and in leveraging the sources for optimum results.

Step 4: Make Adjustments - Now that you have a clear view of your progress, it's time to revisit your strategy. Further amplify the actions contributing to success, rectify mistakes, and make the necessary adjustments to improve your passive income sources' performance. Each adjustment furthers your journey to financial freedom as it means you're making your income sources work better for you.

Step 5: Document Everything - Finally, record all the findings, changes and strategies for future references. Proper documentation aids future direction, serves for comparison in future reviews, and may also become evidence of your achievements on your journey to financial independence.

Remember, this day's tasks are crucial to enhancing your success in passive income generation. They constructively drive you on the path towards financial freedom by continually improving your passive income strategies based on their real-time performance.

As you conclude Day 14 of your journey, be proud of the progress you've made! You are showing tremendous dedication to achieving your financial goals. Keep this momentum going - you are on your way to building your empire. Never underestimate the power of consistency and always remember - your financial future is in your hands!

Day 15

Day 15 revolves around identification of your skills and areas of expertise that can be turned into passive income streams. Here are the detailed steps to help you accomplish this:

1. Skill Audit:
Start your day by conducting an in-depth personal skill audit. Dive deep to identify all your acquired and inherent skills. This can be done by listing down all your job roles over the years and identifying the key skills required for them. Each skill you've developed over the years could potentially be used for passive income generation.

Benefit: Performing a skill audit helps to realize hidden skills that you might have overlooked. These skills can be a great asset in setting up a passive income stream.

2. Prioritization:
Once the skills have been identified, rank them based on your proficiency and passion. The goal is to identify skills that you are not only good at, but also enjoy using. Create a matrix to map each skill on the basis of passion and proficiency.

Benefit: Prioritizing helps in zeroing down on those skills which can be sustained in the long run. A skill you are passionate about is likely going to lead to a more enjoyable and successful passive income venture.

3. Market Research:
Conduct market research to figure out the demand for each of your prioritized skills. Research various online platforms such as Udemy, Coursera, Fiverr, and Upwork, among others to understand what skills are in demand and how your skills can fit into the current marketplace.

Benefit: Understanding the market demand ensures that the skill you decide to monetize has a high potential for earning income. It reduces the risk of starting a venture that won't gain traction.

4. Plan of Action:
Based on the priorities and market research, create a detailed plan of action that outlines how to monetize these skills. This could involve

creating online courses, writing eBooks, or offering freelance services.

Benefit: A plan of action provides a roadmap marking each step to reach your goal. It adds a sense of direction and makes the process less overwhelming.

End the day by revisiting your success so far and acknowledging that you are one step closer to financial freedom. Stay proactive and committed to the journey. Remember, your skills and talents are unique to you and hold immense potential. Stick with it, your path to financial freedom is in progress. Feel proud of the work that you've accomplished! Keep your positive momentum going – you're doing great!

Day 16 - Harnessing Your Skills For Passive Income Generation

Day 16 is all about taking an introspective and analytical journey into your skillset and understanding how these skills can produce income in a passive manner. Here are the detailed steps for Day 16:

Step 1: Self-Assessment: The first important thing you must do is self-assess. Make a list of your professional skills. Include everything from technical abilities, such as knowledge of marketing tools or software programming, to broader competencies like project management, problem-solving, or negotiation. Reflecting on your career to this point, what are the skills that have contributed to your success? Listing every skill, no matter how small, is important at this stage as sometimes the smallest skills can be turned into lucrative passive income sources.

Step 2: Skill Ranking: Rank these skills in accordance with your proficiency level. Which skills could you write a book about? Which ones are you constantly asked to help others with? This will allow you to bring forth your strongest skills that could effortlessly be translated into a source of income.

Step 3: Market Research: Now identify which of your top skills are highly in demand in the market. Use platforms like LinkedIn, job boards, or social media groups to gauge which skills are most sought after. This will help you to understand which skills hold potential to generate consistent passive income.

Step 4: Analyzing the Passive Income Potential: Once you have identified the high-demand skills, plan how can they be turned into a passive income stream. For instance, if your strong suit is digital marketing, you could write an ebook or create an online course sharing your knowledge, both of which can generate passive income once created.

Step 5: Implementation Blueprint: Based on your previous analysis, draft a blueprint of how to leverage your skills. The blueprint will consist of what type of product (like eBooks, courses, or apps) you will develop, what would be its outline, and how you will market this to reach your targeted audience.

Each of these steps is not only important but necessary for successfully generating passive income. Identifying marketable skills and understanding their demand in the market forms the foundation of your passive income journey. Creating a blueprint offers a clear action plan, making the process more manageable and less intimidating, increasing the probability of success.

Remember, your skills and knowledge are valuable assets. They hold the key to financial freedom if used creatively. As Aristotle once said, "The hardest victory is the victory over self, so stay focused, be persistent, and believe in yourself. You are one step closer to financial freedom on your unique journey of passive income generation! Keep going, you got this!

Day 17

On Day 17 of your 30-Day Action Plan for securing financial freedom via passive income, your main task is to outline your platform strategy. Here is a detailed breakdown of your step-by-step tasks:

1. Identify Potential Platforms: Your first task of the day is to brainstorm all possible platforms that align with your skills identified on Day 16. This could include eBook platforms like

Amazon Kindle Direct Publishing, online teaching platforms like Udemy, or freelance websites like Upwork or Fiverr. Identifying these platforms gives you a clear idea of where your skills can be most effectively facilitated and monetized.

2. Research Each Platform: Once you've listed possible platforms, dedicate time to research each one in detail. Look at its popularity, user base, terms and conditions, revenue options, and competition. Understanding these facets helps you comprehend the potential earning power and client base each platform offers.

3. Align Your Skills with Platforms: After researching, align each platform with your skills. For instance, if you're a good writer, Amazon Kindle Direct Publishing might be perfect. If you have teaching skills, consider Udemy. This alignment allows you to optimize your unique skills to generate passive income optimally.

4. Finalize the Platform: Now, make a critical decision and select a single platform, or a couple at most, that you believe will yield the most beneficial results. Remember, the goal is not to scatter yourself thinly over various platforms but instead to master and extract most from one or two.

How does Day 17 help with success for Passive Income for Financial Freedom?

Day 17 is focused on setting the foundation for your passive income stream. Selecting the right platform that complements your skillset is vital for success. Through meticulous research and assessment, you ensure that the platform you select has the potential to harness your expertise most profitably and effectively, setting the stage for future income generation.

Indeed, Day 17 is a valuable step in designing your custom path to financial freedom through passive income. It propels you towards a focused application of your skills, ensuring that your journey towards wealth is rooted in strategic decisions and your distinctive strengths.

Remember, every step you take on this journey, including today's planning and platform selection, is paving the way towards a brighter, financially secure future. Keep going strong, appreciate the progress you're making - every step takes you closer to your goal of financial freedom. The power to create a prosperous life lies within you!

Day 18

Day 18 is a turning point in your journey towards financial freedom. It is the day where you begin to leverage your talents and hone your skills into passive income generation streams.

Step 1: Self-evaluation
Take a deep dive into all your skills, knowledge, and areas of expertise. Reflect on your past job roles, successes, or hobbies. This could be anything ranging from content creation, consultancy, digital marketing, or even baking! The evaluation will help you identify key skill sets that could potentially be monetized.

Step 2: Skill Assessment
Analyze your skills from a commercial point of view. Ask relevant questions such as how these skills bring value to others, do you enjoy utilizing these skills, and more importantly, if these skills have market demand. This assessment is crucial to ensure that your chosen skill has a realistic probability of generating passive income.

Step 3: Market Research
Conduct thorough online research on successful business models based on your skills. Find out what others in the same domain are offering, their pricing structures, and customer feedback. Knowing your marketplace helps to properly position your offerings and understand what potential customers might expect from you.

Step 4: Passive Income Source Ideas Generation
With a good understanding of your skills and the market, brainstorm on ways to turn these skills into a source of passive income. This could be teaching your skills online, writing eBooks or blogs, consulting, or selling crafted products.

Step 5: Narrow Down Your Options
Consider factors like initial investment needed, time commitment, and revenue potential to zero down to the most viable option. This helps ensure that your chosen path aligns with your financial and personal goals.

Now, you've successfully turned your career skills into a potentially profitable model for passive income. The transformation strategy you've begun today is the cornerstone for your journey to financial freedom. It leverages your strengths, aligns them with market needs, and puts you on the path to success.

Remember, everyone has valuable skills. The challenge is to identify them and use them proficiently for value creation. As you go ahead, remember to enjoy the process, celebrate minor victories, and stay unwavering in your commitment. The journey to financial freedom isn't always straightforward, but with a clear focus on your skills and a well-thought-out strategy, you're well on your way to success!

Turning your skills into a passive income source is like turning a formidable seed into a money tree. It may take time, but well-nurtured it will let you reap benefits for a lifetime! Stick to the plan, and success will follow!

Day 19 - Launching Your Passive Income Content Marketing Plan

Day 19 of acquiring passive income for financial freedom requires you to be strategic and analytical. Today, you'll start implementing the marketing plan for your passive income content—whether that's your eBook, online course, freelance services, or blog.

Step 1: Evaluate Your Marketing Plan
Start your day by revisiting your marketing plan, familiarizing yourself with the various components like your target audience, promotional channels, and promotional strategies. Understanding how each element fits into your comprehensive plan to generate passive income is crucial for effective execution.

Step 2: Lay the Foundation

Next, begin with the most basic steps of your plan. It might mean setting up social media accounts for your brand, starting an email list, or establishing connections with influencers who can endorse your content. These foundational steps help build your visibility and audience.

Step 3: Create a Promotional Content Schedule
Develop a detailed, organized content schedule for your promotional activities that includes what you will share, when you will share it, and on what platform. This step ensures consistency on your promotional efforts, which leads to audience trust, a crucial element for passive income success as it fosters recurring income sources and customer loyalty.

Step 4: Implement Your First Promotional Activity
Kickstart your marketing plan's core element, pushing the initial promotional content according to your schedule. Depending on your channel and audience, this could be a catchy social media post, a personalized email, or a beginner's offer.

Step 5: Monitor and Evaluate
The day winds up with monitoring and assessment of the reaction generated by your initial promotional activities. Keeping track of metrics like reach, engagement, and lead generation will yield insight into how your strategy is performing, allowing you to adjust and optimize for the best results.

Day 19 acts as the first real-world test of your passive income efforts. It's the day your product moves from the development phase to the marketplace, facing potential consumers for the first time. Hence, this day holds great significance in laying the foundation for the success of your passive income endeavors by making your presence known, attracting your audience, and starting to build relationships that can lead to continuous income.

Remember, Rome wasn't built in a day, and neither will your passive income stream. It takes time, patience, and resilience. Celebrate the small steps and keep reminding yourself of your ultimate goal: financial freedom. You're doing something incredible here, creating a pathway that leads you to the life you deserve. Hold on to your vision, and keep moving forward with determination. The best is yet to come!

Day 20 - Translating Skills into Action

On Day 20, you will be taking the skills and areas of expertise you've identified and start to outline precise, executable action plans to transform them into sources of passive income.

Step 1: Skills Prioritization

Start your day by organizing and prioritizing the skills you identified on Day 15-17 according to their potential for generating passive income. This could be based on market demand, uniqueness of the skill, and your level of expertise.

Step 2: Market Demand Research

For each of your prioritized skills, conduct a detailed research on market demand. Use platforms like Google Trends, Keyword Planner, or relevant freelance job boards to gauge demand. Understanding what the market needs helps you better position your offerings.

Step 3: Unique Value Proposition

Identify your unique value proposition (UVP) for each skill. What sets you apart from others offering similar skills or services? Maybe you have a unique method of teaching a trade, or perhaps your experience in a niche sector is hard to come by. This distinctiveness can help command a higher price for your offerings.

Step 4: Passive Income Methods Identification

Next, explore the various methods through which you can monetize your skills. For instance, if you're an expert in fitness, you can create an online course, write an e-book, or start a YouTube channel. Being specific in this step helps you take full advantage of your skill set for passive income generation.

Step 5: Action Plan Formulation

Finally, outline a clear, practical action plan for each of your prioritized skills. This should include what platform to use, what content to create, a marketing strategy, and a timeline with clearly defined goals.

Day 20 bridges the idea phase and the action phase of your passive income journey. By the end of the day, you should have a clear understanding of how to turn your career skills into a sustainable passive income strategy.

Remember, making a significant change takes time, effort, and patience. However, once set, passive income sources can yield returns in the long-term, setting you on a path towards financial freedom.

Each step taken today builds on the foundation laid in the past 19 days. You're turning ideas into actions, and this is a significant step in your journey towards financial freedom. Stay persistent and always keep your goals in mind. Every step, no matter how small, is progress, and remember, the future you are working tirelessly towards is worth the effort.

Day 21 - A Feast for Engagement

On the 21st day of your roadmap to financial freedom through passive income, your main objective is to engage with your audience. Here's a step by step guide on how to achieve this:

Step 1: Audience Segregation

The most critical step you can take to successfully engage with your audience is to understand them thoroughly. Segment your audience based on demographics, their interests, location, and other parameters relevant to your product by using analytics from the platform you have chosen or your website.

The success of your passive income stream heavily relies on this step as understanding your audience enables you to target your promotional strategies more efficiently.

Step 2: Respond to Comments and Queries

Keep a close eye on your chosen platform and website for any reactions to your promotional content. Your audience may have questions or comments that should be addressed promptly, genuinely, and professionally. Show interest and interact with them by providing additional information and resolving their queries.

This interaction helps you build a relationship with your audience, making them more likely to invest in your product. It also boosts your credibility and reputation, thereby enhancing the probability of generating and sustaining passive income.

Step 3: Collect Feedback

Always strive to ask for feedback from your audience. Having real interaction and open discussions about your product provides insight into its advantages, disadvantages, and suggestions for improvement.

This step paves the way towards success by promoting perpetual evolution, ensuring that your service or product is always updated with the market's requirements, which further optimises your revenue stream.

Step 4: Public Acknowledgement and Appreciation

Whenever someone provides useful feedback or has a positive response, publicly acknowledge their comment and express appreciation. Recognition of their input not only creates loyalty but can also motivate other audience members to engage more.

This step aids in retaining your audience and amplifies your reach, directly impacting your passive income stream's success.

Step 5: Be Consistent

Engaging with your audience should be a continual process. Do not restrict yourself to just one day of interaction. Remember, consistency is the key to maintaining the attention of your audience and keeps your product in their minds.

Consistency in engagement boosts your image, accelerates sales, and maximizes your passive income revenue.

Ending Day 21 on this note, remember this crucial quote from American author, marketer, and public speaker, Seth Godin, Marketing is no longer about the stuff that you make, but about the stories you tell. So, keep engaging, keep narrating your story, and let's meet back for the next step in realizing your financial freedom. Every step taken in understanding and diving into interaction with your consumer base is a step closer to your goals. Remember, there's virtue in patience and persistence. Let's continue this journey to prosperity, one day at a time!

Day 22 - Laying the Foundations of Mindfulness for Financial Stability

Step 1: Understand the Concept of Mindfulness
Using reliable sources, read up on the concept of mindfulness. Understand that it's a mental state achieved by focusing on the present moment, calmly acknowledging and accepting one's feelings, thoughts, and sensations. This step will form a strong understanding which is crucial for the following steps. It will help you stay focused and reduce impulsive decisions, vital for success in passive income generation.

Step 2: Acknowledge your Current Financial Status
While focusing on your breathing, reflect upon your current financial status. Be honest in acknowledging your debts, savings, investments, income sources. The purpose here isn't to invite stress, but to form an objective view of your financial reality. This acceptance enables effective planning for passive income ventures.

Step 3: Visualize your Financial Goals

Close your eyes and create a mental image of your financial freedom. Visualize your goals as realities, like, the passive income sources effectively functioning, and the comfort and peace coming with it. This sets a clear destination, keeps you motivated and focused on your passive income goals.

Step 4: Practice Mindfulness Meditation
Look for a simple 10-minute guided mindfulness meditation video online and follow along. Pay attention to breath, thoughts, and emotions. Regular practice of mindfulness meditation can reduce anxiety caused by financial concerns, improving mental health and focus in your journey towards financial freedom.

Step 5: Journal your Insights
Finish your mindfulness session by journaling any insights or decisions made during the practice. This serves as a handy reference for future and helps keep track of your progress towards financial freedom.

Understanding and practicing mindfulness can play a potent role when it comes to wealth-building. It improves your decision-making abilities, increases your focus, and provides emotional stability, which are critical for managing your passive income sources and achieving financial freedom.

With the newly adopted mindfulness practice, you are advancing further on the path of financial freedom. The journey to wealth creation may not always be smooth, but remember, every step forward, no matter how small, is a step towards achieving your goal. You have been doing fantastic work up till now, and I encourage you to stay engaged, patient, and persistent as you continue on this journey, no matter the challenges you may face. Keep going, success comes to those who persevere!

Day 23 - Developing Mindfulness Strategies

On Day 23, your focus is on developing mindfulness strategies applicable to your personal financial situation. Mindfulness is a psychological practice that brings attention to the present time, which can aid in making rational and beneficial financial decisions.

Step 1: Morning Meditation
Start your day with a 10-minute meditation, focusing on your breath. This can help clear your mind and begin your day with enhanced concentration and focus.

Step 2: Gain Knowledge
Familiarize yourself with financial mindfulness. Spend some time reading on financial mindfulness techniques. Listen to podcasts or watch videos to deepen your understanding.

Step 3: Identify Stressors
Next, identify the primary stress points in your financial strategy. These could be worries about investments not paying off, anxiety over portfolio management, or concern about retirement savings. Recognizing these stressors is essential to develop strategies to effectively manage them.

Step 4: Mindful Reflection
Reflect on each of your financial stressors individually. Consider each stressor carefully and mindfully without judgment, but rather, with acceptance and a willingness to address it. This understanding can help build resilience and equanimity in your financial journey.

Step 5: Develop Strategies
Based on your reflections, develop a personalized mindfulness strategy for each identified financial stressor. This could range from setting aside specific worry-free times during your day, using mindfulness to interrupt mental loops about financial worries, or making a commitment to handle financial tasks at scheduled times only.

Step 6: Practice
Begin to practice these strategies in low-stress situations first. This allows you to get comfortable with the practice before applying it to higher-stress scenarios.

Day 23 enables you to focus on mental and emotional stability. By introducing mindfulness into your financial strategy, you're not just aiming for monetary gain but a holistic prosperity that includes peace of mind. This tranquility allows you to make thoughtful, composed decisions, instead of knee-jerk reactions which can not only cost you money but also disrupt the calmness necessary to remain financially focused and resilient.

Remember, your journey towards financial freedom is unique, so your mindfulness strategy should also be tailor-made. You're doing great! Keep in mind that the progress you make each day brings you one step closer to your goals for achieving financial freedom. Each stride, no matter how little, counts. Keep going, you've got this!

Day 24

On Day 24 of your journey towards financial freedom, you are going to develop specific mindfulness strategies applicable to your personal financial scenario. This important step is geared towards forging an enduring link between your financial ambitions and mental resilience. Let's dive into the details:

Step#1: Identify your Financial Stressors (1-2 hours)
The first task of Day 24 involves reflection and introspection. Identify aspects of your financial life that cause stress or concern. It may be the fear of financial instability, the unease of investment risks, or simply the pressure to succeed. The aim is to clearly define these stressors so you can address them with mindfulness.

How it helps: Understanding your stressors helps you recognize triggers that may affect your decision-making process, blend emotional resilience into your financial strategies, and free your mind to identify and seize opportunities for passive income generation.

Step#2: Develop Mindfulness Strategies (2-3 hours)
Based on your identified stressors, develop at least 3 mindfulness strategies. These strategies may include grounding exercises (where

you bring your focus to what's physically around you), guided visualisation (where you imagine a peaceful scene or outcome), and/or daily meditation or affirmations.

How it helps: These strategies are designed to reduce anxiety, boost mental clarity, and promote a more balanced approach to financial decision-making; facets that are crucial for successfully managing passive income streams and achieving financial freedom.

Step#3: Document your findings (1 hour)
Record your stressors and corresponding mindfulness strategies meticulously in a journal or a digital app. This exercise ensures you have a clear understanding and an easy reference for times of financial turbulence.

How it helps: Documenting these strategies gives you a ready reckoner to turn to in times of stress. It guarantees that the strategies are at your fingertips, readily accessible whenever needed, thereby maintaining a calm, focused mind to successfully manage your passive income sources.

Step#4: Practice a Chosen Mindfulness Strategy (1 hour)
Finally, spend the last part of the day putting one of your chosen mindfulness strategies into practice. This could be meditation, deep-breathing exercises, or even yoga.

How it helps: 'Practicing what you preach' reinforces your commitment. This real-time experience enables you to cleanse your thoughts, enhance focus, and prime your mind towards successful passive income management.

Remember, the endeavor of achieving financial freedom is just as much a test of mental endurance as it is of strategic planning. Mindfulness grants you the serenity and clarity required to successfully manage your passive income ventures.

So, at the end of Day 24, accustom yourself to implement mindfulness in your financial sphere. With your newfound mental strength, no financial goal will seem unattainable! Keep embracing this learning curve and remember - the view gets better as you ascend. Let's keep climbing to the peak of financial freedom together!

Day 25 – Fine-tuning content based on audience feedback

On day 25, your task is to fine-tune your content according to the feedback gained from your audience. Remember, passive income relies heavily on the value you provide to your audience, and any insights you gain from them are a goldmine for improving your offerings.

Here's your step-by-step guide for Day 25:

Step 1: Review Feedback

Start your day by going through all comments, emails, or reviews where your audience has provided any feedback on your initial content or promotional strategies. This includes social media platforms, email responses, comment sections of your blogs, or any other forum where you interact with your audience.

The crux of this step is to understand your audience's opinions on the value your content provides and to identify what they felt was missing. This step is critical for making your content more valuable and, therefore, more profitable in creating passive income.

Step 2: Summarize Insights

Once you've noted down all feedback, compile these insights into a single document. Look for recurring themes or suggestions - these are the areas that your audience is most interested in seeing improved.

By summarizing your insights, you can easily map out the path to take for better audience engagement, which will result in more passive income. Your goal here is to maximize the value your content offers through your audience's perspective.

Step 3: Modify your Content

Now that you have a comprehensive list of areas to improve, start modifying your content. This could mean revising your ebook, adding relevant sections to your online courses, or enhancing your affiliate marketing content.

The goal is to create a more engaging, value-packed, and user-focused content that entices your audience to invest their time and money in what you have to offer. Remember, your content should not only provide information but also convince your audience that their investment is worth it.

Step 4: Announce Amendments

Once your changes are in place, share the modifications with your audience. Your post should point out that you listened to their feedback and adjusted the content accordingly. This cultivates a sense of community and assures them that their voice matters.

Sharing this shows the transparency of your process and builds trust with your audience, fostering greater loyalty and eventually boosting your passive income streams.

Step 5: Implement

Lastly, upload your revised content onto your platform. Monitor closely the reactions and feedback moving forward, it's a continuous process of adjusting for success.

At this stage of your 30-day plan, each day is a step closer to financial freedom. You are harnessing the power of passive income, and every refinement you make keep adding to that momentum. Remember, the secret to building wealth through passive income is patience, persistence, and continuous improvement. You've got this! Keep moving forward, confident in the knowledge that you're capable of creating a successful, financially independent future!

Day 26 - Mindfulness Practice and Financial Freedom

Step 1: Early Morning Mindfulness Meditation

Start your day with a mindfulness meditation session of at least 20 minutes. Find a quiet, peaceful spot, sit comfortably, close your eyes, and focus your mind on your breathing. This step of mindfulness meditation helps to center your thoughts and emotions, clearing away any anxiety or stress that could affect your financial decisions.

Step 2: Review Your Personal Portfolio
After mentally preparing yourself, review your current portfolio. By reviewing your portfolio with a calm and focused mind, you can make more rational and balanced decisions, which is a prerequisite for a successful passive income strategy.

Step 3: Daily Financial Mindfulness Journaling
Take out your financial mindfulness journal. Write down your reflections about your current financial situation, your passive income sources, and how you feel about them. This step helps to create a clearer understanding of your financial status and provides insights into how your attitudes and emotions might be influencing your financial decisions.

Step 4: Visualize Financial Freedom
Take a few moments to visualize your financial freedom. Think about the peace and security it will bring to your life. This practice contributes to maintaining your motivation and commitment to the goal, encouraging you to continue in your financial freedom journey.

Step 5: Mindful Decision-Making Practice
Engage in a practice session of mindfulness-based decision making related to financial scenarios. This could be around decisions concerning investments, spending, or saving. Play out different scenarios and observe your thoughts without judgment. This reflective practice can significantly improve your intuitive ability to make financially beneficial decisions in the future.

Step 6: Evening Mindfulness Reflection
End the day with a mindfulness reflection on the day's activities and your financial decisions. It's crucial to assess the day's successes and

challenges, which will lead to better financial decisions, and thus, greater passive income.

Day 26 is crucial because it bridges the gap between your financial goals and the emotional intelligence needed to achieve them. Each step of this day is designed to improve your mental and emotional well-being while simultaneously honing your financial decision-making skills. Incorporating mindfulness into your financial strategy positions you to create and manage passive income sources for financial freedom more effectively.

Remember, every step taken is a step closer to financial freedom. You are doing great, and with patience, persistence, and mindfulness, you are bound to achieve your goal. Keep going!

Day 27 - Mindful Practices for Harmony in Financial Affairs

Day 27 is devoted to integrating your mindfulness exercises into your daily routine. This would allow you to manage your financial resources better and make more informed decisions leading to optimal passive income generation and financial freedom.

Step 1: Morning Meditation

Begin your day with a 10-15 minute meditation. Opt for guided meditations that focus on abundance and gratitude. This will set the tone for the day, encouraging a positive mindset and an awareness of the wealth being created and the opportunities that lie ahead.

Step 2: Financial Affirmations

Next, take a moment to articulate daily financial affirmations. These positive statements will reinforce your financial goals and ambitions. Be as specific as possible, for example, I am successfully creating multiple streams of passive income, or I am confidently making wise investment decisions. This step will stimulate a positive belief system, essential for financial success.

Step 3: Mindful Evaluation of Investments

Allocate a certain portion of your day to consciously evaluate your investments. Apply the mindfulness techniques you've been practicing to remain calm and clear-headed as you scrutinize your financial decisions. Observe without judgment, noting your emotional responses, and questioning if they are influencing your decisions. Being mindful will prevent rash, emotion-driven financial decisions.

Step 4: Gratitude Journaling

At the end of your day, take few minutes to jot down your financial wins, no matter how small. This form of gratitude journaling brings awareness to incremental success and keeps your momentum going. You'll appreciate your progress and stay motivated to keep going.

Step 5: Evening Reflection

As you wind down, reflect on your day, recognizing patterns in your behavior, thoughts, or feelings concerning your financial activities. This is about understanding how your mind works, which gives you greater control over your responses to financial situations, helping to maintain clarity and composure even in times of volatility or uncertainty.

Each of these steps contributes to a coherent mindset, fosters a positive attitude towards wealth generation, and encourages responsible decision-making. The practices leverage the power of the mind towards achieving your goals of passive income generation and financial freedom.

Stay the course, your commitment to this plan is a testament to your determination. Remember, building wealth is a journey, not a sprint. You're investing in your financial future and each step brings you closer to your financial freedom.

Day 28 - Evaluating Progress and Redefining Goals

Day 28 focuses on assessing the stride you have made towards your passive income goals, identifying gaps, and formulating strategies to optimize performance.

Step 1: Analyze Key Performance Indicators (KPIs)
Start the day by checking the KPIs for each of your passive income ventures. These might include things like number of eBook sales, online course enrollments, or the return on investment from your investment portfolio, among others. This meticulous analysis benefits you by providing visible metrics that indicate how well your ventures are performing in relation to your projected targets.

Step 2: Reflect on Your Achievements and Shortcomings
After examining the KPIs, take some time to reflect on what they mean. Identify which goals have been met, are in progress, or have fallen short. Make a list of successes and disappointments. This honest and reflective practice aids in understanding your accomplishments, determining where corrections or adjustments need to be made, and encouraging you to strive for more.

Step 3: Redefine Goals and Strategies
Once you list down your achievements and shortcomings, redefine your goals and tweak your strategies based on the insights gained. For instance, if your eBook sales have exceeded expectations, you might decide to produce more eBooks. Conversely, if your online course enrollments are below expectations, you might need to reassess your marketing approach or revisit course content. This step ensures you keep evolving and adapting to always perform at your best.

Step 4: Plan for The Upcoming Days
The last task of the day is to set the tone for the next couple of days. Based on the updated goals and strategies, plan out actionable tasks, anticipating possible challenges, and prepare to tackle them. This helps you begin the following days with clarity and purpose.

Day 28 serves an invaluable role in your journey towards financial freedom. By forcing you to confront your performance, it ensures that you remain aware, adaptable, and resilient. It provides an excellent chance not only to celebrate accomplishments but more importantly to learn from the downfalls. Understanding the need for periodic evaluation and adjustment paves the way towards sustained success in realizing passive income goals.

Remember, the journey towards financial freedom is not always smooth sailing. There would be days when you exceed expectations and days when things don't go as planned. Yet, every step, every stumble, and every leap you take brings you closer to your goal. Keep showing up, keep refining your strategies, and most importantly, keep believing in your capacity to achieve financial freedom. You're doing great! Press on.

Day 29 - Ongoing Audience Engagement and Community Building

The penultimate day of your 30-day action plan for passive income generation is focused on an essential, yet often overlooked aspect of financial freedom: audience engagement and community building. Here are the granular steps involved:

Step 1: Respond to Everything
Begin your day by addressing every correspondence that may have accumulated overnight. This could be comments or queries on your social media channels, feedback on your products or services, or emails from potential leads. This makes your audience feel heard and valued.

Step 2: Content Creation
Create some sort of valuable additional content related to your passive income source to share with your audience. This could be a blog post, infographic or a short video. The purpose is to continue providing value and keeping your audience engaged.

Step 3: Promotion
Share your created content across your preferred channels. Use planned promotion strategies to ensure maximum reach. This helps not only in attracting new potential customers but maintaining the interest of current ones, which is essential for sustainable passive income.

Step 4: Organize a Community Activity
Organize a community activity, such as an online webinar, Q&A session, or a poll. This encourages interaction within your audience,

strengthens community bonds, and boosts the popularity of your passive income venture.

Step 5: Analyze Feedback
At the end of the day, analyze the feedback and interaction from your audience on the shared content and activity. This provides insights into the audience's preferences, helping you tailor future products or services.

Step 6: Plan for Tomorrow
Based on today's feedback, identify areas for improvement, and plan your activities for the next day. This continual optimization ensures that your passive income stream remains relevant and lucrative.

Engaging your audience proactively, maintaining a lively community, and ensuring their queries and feedback don't fall on deaf ears is absolutely critical to your success. It builds brand loyalty, encourages repeat business, and creates a sense of trust and credibility among your audience – all essential ingredients for a steady, passive income source.

As we approach the end of this 30-day journey, remember that nothing worth having comes easy. Don't forget that even though this process challenging, the reward – financial freedom – is absolutely worth the effort. As long as you remain focused, committed and smart in your decision-making, financial liberty isn't just a possibility, it's an inevitability. Keep going, you're almost there!

Day 30 - Evaluation and Expansion

The ultimate day of your 30-day action plan is intended to consolidate your passive income strategies and emphasize the importance of continuous improvement and consistent application.

Step 1: Revision and Reflection
Start your day by revisiting all the actions, strategies, and decisions you've implemented over the course of the past 29 days. This reflection helps you gain a bird's eye view of your journey towards financial freedom, allowing you to discern patterns and identify areas of success and opportunity.

Step 2: KPI Evaluation
Assess your Key Performance Indicators (KPIs). This is a crucial step as it quantifies your progress and effectiveness, allowing you to gauge how well you're matching up to the SMART goals you've set. This ties directly into your success in passive income as accurate tracking can highlight your best-performing income sources, thus enabling strategic investment and expansion.

Step 3: Action Plan Review
Literally, go through your action plan you've developed in Week 3. Evaluate the listed role of your career skills in generating a passive income. Ensure you've utilized these skills in your chosen platform effectively for maximum gain.

Step 4: Mindfulness Exercise
Engage in a mindfulness exercise. This practice entails the techniques you've developed on Day 22-26, serving as your emotional and mental stability anchor. The correlation between stability and financial success is significant, as maintaining a clear head and calm demeanor can contribute heavily to better decision-making and long-term, consistent growth.

Step 5: Comparative Study
With all the data gathered, perform a comparative study of all the passive income paths you've undertaken. Identify the best-performing venture, consider the reasons explaining its success, and plan out how to further its expansion.

Step 6: Next Steps Planning
Finally, based on the results of your most successful passive income venture, plan for the next set of actions. This could mean ramping up your investment or increasing your focus on a particular skill set.

Every step contributes to your financial freedom success. Revision enables you to avoid past mistakes. KPI evaluation identifies successful income routes, and mindfulness keeps you grounded and resilient. A comparative study helps you understand what works best, making future endeavors more successful.

Remember that this is not the end of your journey, but a significant milestone. The key to sustainable financial freedom is constant progress, not perfection. Keep moving forward, carry the lessons you've learned, and always be open to growth and new opportunities. Keep on this path, and you'll find that financial freedom isn't just reachable—it's maintainable. Your journey to financial abundance is a testament to your diligence, and we're right here, cheering you on as you forge ahead to even greater heights. Remember this; the quest for financial liberation is not a sprint, but a marathon. Every step, no matter how small, is a step forward. Onward and upward!

CHAPTER 13: SUCCESS STORIES:WALKING THE ROAD TO SUCCESS

A Journey Unveiled

A year ago, I began reading the book, 30 Day Action Plan for Success, with curiosity and excitement. Developing multiple streams of passive income was a goal I'd been dreaming about but didn't know where to begin. The book provided not just inspirational anecdotes, but a concrete step-by-step formula to achieve my dreams.

As directed, I started doing market research to identify sources of passive income. I selected real estate, creating a blog, and stock investments as my three main sources. Allocating resources and developing strategies for each, I found the book being instrumental in helping me realize how realistic and attainable those goals were.

When I started implementing my strategies, I'll confess, some days were tough. I had lots of learning to do, hit some challenges with time management, and experienced the occasional setback in the stock market, but I kept revising my strategies and moving forward, just as the guide implored.

In addition to these three areas, I also explored my professional skills which I found I could monetize. Being a programmer, I realized that I could create an online course out of my knowledge, as suggested on Day 15 of the book.

Fast-forward to now, my real estate investments have started yielding rentals; my blog attracts enough traffic to make revenues from ads, and my stocks have started to regain their value. But one of my biggest achievements has been the success of my online course which has allowed me to connect with thousands while generating a significant income.

In the end, not only did the 30 Day Action Plan for Success motivate me and guide me, but it provided an executable blueprint from which I've created a consistent earnings stream. The different steps not only unfolded a clear path but allowed me to learn, grow, and adapt, making my journey towards financial independence a highly empowering experience. This book is a must-read for anyone seriously contemplating unveiling their potential.

A Journey to Financial Independence: Mark's Success Story with the 30 Day Action Plan

When Mark first picked up the '30 Day Action Plan for Success', he was in a rut professionally. Mark's corporate job was beginning to drain him, and he longed for an income stream that required less input from him yet significantly increased his revenue. He knew that passive income was the key, but he never really understood how to go about it until he got his hands on this book.

The first 14 days of the action plan were quite an enlightening roller coaster for him. It guided him to identify his potential passive income streams, conduct in-depth analysis, and finally choose three diverse options - stock investment, a tech blog, and an online store for homemade candles.

Mark was smart enough to choose options that align with his skills and interests. He had a basic understanding of the stock market, he was tech-savvy, and he enjoyed making candles. This indeed played an essential role in keeping his motivation levels high. The investment strategy formulation was a novel concept which proved to be a game-changer for Mark.

Implementing the plan for each income source was thrilling. He could see his theoretical knowledge shaping into something substantial, and the progress monitoring helped him understand the dynamic nature of passive income sources.

From Day 15, the journey became even more interesting as he explored monetizing his professional skills. With a background in project management, he decided to create a Project Management e-course. The creation and marketing aspects were challenging but fulfilling.

Within a month of launching his online course, he had more than 200 students enrolled! Plus, his blog began generating ad revenue, and his candle store started catching attention. He continues to engage with his audience, collect feedback, and make necessary changes.

Mark has translated his skills and interests into substantial passive income streams following the 30 Day Action Plan. Today, he shares his success story to motivate everyone who wants to achieve financial independence. As Mark puts it, The prime success factor is indeed the structure and clarity that the '30 Day Action Plan for Success' offers. It takes you on a detail-oriented, goal-driven, and result-oriented journey which I would strongly recommend to anyone aiming for a different kind of financial freedom.

From Frantic to Financial Freedom: A Silent Success Story

Jeff Atwood, a middle-grade consultant within a multinational corporation, was living the chaotic life of constantly juggling responsibilities and targets while leading a team. The stress and demands of climbing up the corporate ladder seemed to leave him no time to live and enjoy his present. He felt a need for change, a need for more control over his life and financial stability.

Being a follower of self-help and financial success books, Jeff stumbled upon my 30 Day Action Plan for Success, a guide designed to help individuals create and manage passive income sources. Always driven and enthusiastic, Jeff decided to commit himself to the fully outlined 30-day action program.

During the initial week, Jeff learnt to select passive income sources that align with his interests and skills. As a passionate horticulture enthusiast, he decided upon setting up a niche blog, investing in agri-related stocks, and creating an e-book on beginner's guide to urban farming. He planned his investments meticulously and kept an accurate record of each penny he spent and earned.

Using the strategies and tips mentioned in the book, Jeff started to see potential profits in just two weeks. His blog started receiving a steady stream of organic traffic and the e-book demand was higher than he ever anticipated. His small stock investments were beginning to multiply, slowly yet steadily.

By following the book's advice, Jeff created a strong bonding with his audience. His workshops, where he demonstrated his green thumb, became popular and even attracted some local sponsors. Jeff's blog, which started as merely a passion project, now brings him a sizeable advertising and sponsorship income.

Jeff's e-book, "The Ultimate Urban Farming Guide for Beginners", was a resounding success. Thanks to the promotional strategies he had learned, it not only sold well but also positioned him as a knowledgeable authority in the field.

By the end of the 30-day plan, Jeff had several passive income streams that aligned perfectly with his passion and skills. He greatly reduced his stress and enjoyed both a new-found financial freedom and a deeply satisfying passion-cum-business venture. Jeff was able to achieve a rewarding work-life balance that he used to only dream about.

Jeff's steady and relentless method of following the 30 Day Action Plan for Success proved how an ordinary individual can achieve extraordinary results. It's a real-world testament to the roadmap provided in the book and gives hopefuls a proven path to tread on their journey to financial success. His story is truly inspirational to all the dreamers who wish to break free from financial concerns and live a fulfilling life.

CONCLUSION

The '30 Day Action Plan for Success' is your comprehensive guide towards financial independence and a holistic investment strategy. Each day in this plan signifies a step closer to your dream of creating multiple income streams and leveraging your skills to generate smart revenues.

The journey might seem daunting at first, but remember, Rome was not built in a day. Similarly, passive income sources won't blossom overnight. They require careful planning, execution, constant nurturing, and iterative refinement. But hold fast to your vision. Your actions today are the seeds you sow for a sweet harvest tomorrow.

The beauty lies in the starting. Once you commence and build momentum, you'll find your rhythm and discover more about your strengths and potentials than ever before. It's time, dear reader, not only to dream about financial independence but to live it!

Embrace this 30-day challenge with an open mind and heart. Face the challenges, celebrate the successes, and most importantly, appreciate the journey. For it is during this journey that you'll come across your strengths, passions, and enduring resilience.

Brace yourself to transition from mere dreaming to solid action. This 30-day journey is a glide path to your richer self. Remember, every step counts and only those who dare to begin, can hope to finish.

Gear up. Today is the day you start steering your financial future. Let confidence, patience, and diligence guide you. Here's to your 30-day journey to financial freedom, self-discovery, and unimagined success. Begin today, for the future waits for no one. You are the author of your story. Make it a best-seller.

Carpe Diem! Seize your day. Create your path to success today. It's time for you to step into the world of financial independence. The world is yours to conquer, let's get started!

RESOURCES

The purpose of this chapter is to furnish readers with an array of resources and tools aimed at enhancing their understanding of passive income for financial freedom. It's specifically designed for those who are enthusiastic about autonomously building, scaling, and diversifying their income streams. These resources provide detailed knowledge, reliable guidance, important tips, and real-life success stories to inspire and illuminate the path towards financial independence.

Books:

1. Rich Dad Poor Dad by Robert Kiyosaki - An essential read on understanding the importance and the process of making money work for you.

2. Passive Income: Highly Effective Ways To Achieve Wealth Using These Successful Methods by Robert AAron Anglises - Inspires readers to embark on their journey towards financial freedom through multiple passive income avenues.

3. The 4-Hour Workweek by Timothy Ferriss - Ferriss guides the reader on escaping the 9-5 grind while enjoying high income through unique and creative methods.

Articles:

1. "7 Streams of Passive Income To Maintain Your Wealth" – A Forbes article that breaks down the available passive income strategies and how to use them effectively.

2. Passive Income: How to Earn More and Work Less – An article by Investopedia, detailing what passive income is and the numerous ways one can generate it.

Websites:

1. NerdWallet: A dependable resource for practical advice, calculators, and facts about investing and creating productive income.

2. Investopedia: A well-rounded website for financial news, investing terms and definitions, and detailed how-to guides.

Additional Tools:

1. Udemy course – "Passive income for beginners": A comprehensive online course that guides to understand, create, and manage multiple passive income streams.

2. Podcast – "Smart Passive Income" with Pat Flynn: Flynn shares his own experiences and interviews experts in the field of passive income, offering advice on how to avoid common pitfalls.

3. Seminars/Webinars – Events organised by financial advisors, investment experts who share secrets and strategies for generating passive income.

PARTING REFLECTION

Dear friend,

Congratulations on the monumental progress you've already made by embarking on this transformative voyage of financial freedom and personal fulfillment. The courage and resolve to design your life on your own terms, awakened with 'Empowered Pathways: Curating Success on Your Own Terms', is truly commendable. And now, through the synergistic strategies offered in 'Integrated Pathways to Wealth,' you've started manifesting a tangible reality of prosperity and happiness.

Your sagacity in understanding the concept of diversified investing, implementing a dynamic career approach focused on passive income generation, and unlocking inner wealth has been phenomenal. You've successfully created a mechanism that not only generates regular income streams but also aligns with your personal fulfillment and life goals— a masterpiece steeped in financial prudence and relentless passion.

The journey to wealth, especially the route you've taken, is an uncommon one. It bears witness to your unique understanding of market dynamics, your risk management skills, and most importantly, your determination to navigate your career to align with passive income generation. You've proved that wealth creation isn't merely a monetary journey but a process deeply entwined with our aspirations and emotional state.

The power of passive income, as you've wisely adopted, is a game-changer. It's a step towards financial liberation, an antidote to economic uncertainties, and a reliable path towards sustainable growth. By proactively designing multiple streams of passive income, you've fortified your financial future and initiated a cycle of wealth that isn't merely transactional but transformative.

In closing, let me echo the golden words of Wanda Sykes, Success is the sweetest revenge. Your achievements thus far testify to your potential and herald a future replete with larger victories. The journey may be challenging, yet the rewards are undeniably worthwhile. So, keep pushing, keep evolving, keep succeeding.

Remember, you are not just carving a path to wealth; you are shaping a life that speaks of success, satisfaction, and self-made triumphs. As you continue your journey, may the successes you've enjoyed thus far serve as steppingstones to the glittering pinnacle of prosperity that awaits you.

Your friend in success,
Ahjan Samvara